# WARNING:
## Dying May Be Hazardous to Your Wealth

### How to Protect Your Life Savings for Yourself and Those You Love

**By Adriane G. Berg, Esq.**

THE (
180
P
HAWTHO. , ... 07507
1-800-CAREER-1
201-427-0229 (OUTSIDE U.S.)
FAX: 201-427-2037

## WARNING: DYING MAY BE HAZARDOUS TO YOUR WEALTH

### ISBN 1-56414-014-8, $14.95

Cover design by A Good Thing Inc.

Copies of this book may be ordered by mail or phone directly from the publisher. To order by mail, please include price as noted above, $2.50 handling per order, plus $1.00 for each book ordered. (New Jersey residents please add 7% sales tax.) Send to: The Career Press Inc., 180 Fifth Avenue., PO Box 34, Hawthorne, NJ 07507.

Or call Toll-Free 1-800-CAREER-1 to order using your VISA or Mastercard or for further information on all titles published or distributed by Career Press.

---

# Attention: Schools, Organizations, Corporations

This book is available at quantity discounts for bulk purchases for educational, business or sales promotional use.
Please contact: Gretchen Fry,
Career Press, 180 Fifth Avenue
Hawthorne, NJ 07507
or call 1-800-CAREER-1

---

## Acknowledgement

Many thanks to Mark Laifer, my colleague and senior trusts and estates partner, in the law firm of Friedland, Fishbein, Laifer and Robbins, New York City, and to the planned giving division of the United Church of Christ for the use of their excellent materials on charitable giving.

*Dedicated to my wonderful mother (Gramma G.) and her marvelous grandchildren, Arthur Ross Berg Bochner and Rose Phoebe Berg Bochner.*

# CONTENTS

# INTRODUCTION

---

## "The future ain't what it used to be"—Yogi Berra

---

As I travel around the United States giving lectures on estate planning, I am aware of three astonishing trends.

First, there is an ever-growing number of people who are concerned with and are concentrating on preserving their estates for their loved ones. Widows who could hardly balance a checkbook when their husbands died are talking with authority about avoiding probate, making trusts, and executing health care proxies. Business people are exploring the best way to hand over the helm. And young couples are making wills at earlier ages.

Second, everyone is worried about the cost of our longevity. "There's good news and bad news," I say at my seminars. "The good news is you are going to live longer. The bad news is you can't afford to."

The life expectancy for all of us is rising rapidly. From age 46.4 for men and 49 for women at the turn of the century, to 71.4 for men and 78.9 for women in 1990—as calculated by the most conservative statistics from the National Institute on Aging. By the turn of the next century, for every teenager you will see in the mall, there will be *five* senior citizens!

7

People are thinking about their health insurance, Medicaid eligibility and medical treatment with one goal in mind. They want to be able to control their lives and their assets no matter how long they live and no matter what the state of their health. This is true even if control means "pulling the plug" or having a trusted loved one handle their assets.

And, finally, the third trend I've discovered is most troubling: People realize that something fundamental and frightening has happened to the American middle class. The future is, indeed, not what it used to be. We do not have the feeling of prosperity and ever-expanding affluence that we experienced for the past 50 years. Each generation must be ever more careful to preserve its assets for the next.

Senior wealth is a fundamental family asset today. But it is under attack. A study by the Harvard Medical School discovered that of those 75 and older, 46 percent would be impoverished after 13 weeks in a nursing home. At the end of two years, 80 percent to 90 percent would have spent all their accumulated lifetime earnings.

If the nursing home doesn't get you, the tax man will. Without the know-how of the long-time rich, more than 55 percent of your assets could go to federal estate taxes. Taking inflation into consideration, a senior could be leaving his or her heirs only 40 percent of the legacy anticipated, even before the costs of probate are deducted.

In another time we might have developed a philosophy about this. "The children can fend for themselves; leave them well-educated and they will make it from scratch." But we can no longer count on ever-increasing wealth. In fact, today's college generation has a harder time than the prior generation in paying for school and finding jobs. Today's youngest baby boomers are not likely to enjoy as prosperous a lifestyle as their parents. We read about the numbers of adults in their 20s and 30s who are returning to the nest because they can't afford the high cost of living. In many homes, senior wealth is the backbone of the family's hope for the next generation.

## You don't have to be a millionaire to need estate-planning knowledge.

## Introduction

Within the next two generations, we may have to say good-bye to the American middle class as we know it. The American middle class is distinguished by its expectations, ambitions and hopes. These are changing rapidly. And as *they* do, we change profoundly as a people. We also lose a power base that has blessed the average American with more education, prosperity and wealth than most kings in history. What's happening?

1. More than 76 million Americans will reach the age of 65 in the same year—2011, only 19 years from now.
2. Social Security will be drained.
3. The American working class has already failed to contribute enough Social Security to provide for their elders.
4. Middle-class baby boomers are not reproducing at a rate that matches the poor.
5. The situation results in an ever-increasing tax on the middle class to support programs for the poor.
6. While federal education dollars are allocated for families earning under $10,000, 1991 was the first year that middle-class students accepted by the school of their choice could not afford to attend.
7. Objective studies show that only the very rich and very poor are attending the schools of their choice.
8. The average American will live to 74, long enough to watch his or her life savings depleted by the costs of longevity and health care.
9. The middle class must become poor to be eligible for Medicaid.
10. Those 40 to 55 can no longer rely on the resale value of their homes, which has plummeted, to finance their retirement years.
11. Corporate and professional workers have no job security and not enough time to replace what they lost in the recession.

These conclusions come from studies of the United States government, universities and recognized authorities. You know they are true just by looking at your own family and those of your friends. When I lecture, I get 500 heads nodding "no" when I ask participants whether they expect their children to be better off than they are.

Next-generation advancement is the dream that brought every immigrant and some of our finest citizens to this country. Today, the American middle class is witnessing the demise of this dream.

Despite all these trends, we still don't have a grasp on the enormous need to plan for our futures—and the futures of generations to come! No public school teaches it, no mass media advertises it, families find it hard to discuss, professionals are confused as to their roles.

Yet, every middle class American family needs to know how to estate plan. What is estate planning? Getting your money to the people you want to benefit—your family. Preserving your assets from waste through unreasonable taxation and administrative costs. Saving your family the heartbreak of internal fights over money. Saving your family the work of wearing administrative details. Preparing yourself for the new longevity so you can keep your money even if you have a long, expensive illness. Entrusting your money management to the right party in the event you become incompetent. Protecting your spouse from pressure from family members, professionals and creditors. Building fair relationships in first and second marriages and among siblings with different financial lifestyles.

For these reasons and more, estate planning is an essential link in providing for the prosperity of your future and your family's future.

**This book gives every family—and every individual—the knowledge and power to plan for financial well-being now and in the generations to come. I'm sure you can understand it all, no matter who you are:**

- Baby boomer couples creating a college fund.

- Widows and widowers with too little income and taxable estate.
- Older couples with real estate or family business that will go on distress sale to pay taxes.
- Traditional couples who will have no tax when the first one dies, but will pay *thousands* in taxes when the second one dies.
- Couples who are finding their children in their 30s in poor financial shape.
- Divorced persons who must provide for two families in a discreet and economical manner.
- Parents with an incompetent adult child.
- Middle-class families who are afraid of tax and inflationary erosion of wealth.
- Adult children of elderly parents facing catastrophic illnesses.
- Individuals and couples who want to look forward to a comfortable retirement—and leave something to their children.
- Anyone who thinks estate planning is too complicated for them to understand.
- Unmarried couples, gay or heterosexual, who want to provide for each other.
- Anyone who wants to avoid probate and make things easier for their family.
- Anyone who wants to make gifts to their family in the most effective way.
- Every beneficiary of an existing estate plan who wants to understand their rights and perhaps enhance them.
- People who want to provide insurance benefits for their loved ones.
- People with charitable giving in mind.
- *You—for your own good and personal reasons!*

This book will teach you no-risk, well-established estate planning concepts in simple-to-understand language. The concepts can be implemented immediately through attorneys, insurance brokers, planners and by you and your family itself. While the advice is by no means exotic, you may be amazed at the simple devices that can save a family from downward mobility.

Here are some of the estate-planning strategies this book will teach you:

**Dynasty planning**—How to use a small amount of money today to build wealth, tax free, for generations to come.

**Legacy planning**—How a couple can economically build great wealth for children and grandchildren.

**Traditional estate planning**—Essential concepts in a nutshell.

**Probate avoidance**—How avoiding probate costs can leave your family with more.

**Tax planning for the middle class couple**—How little-known strategies can easily save nearly $200,000 in taxes.

**Tax planning for widows and widowers**—How tactics used almost exclusively by the rich can save a legacy and also give the single person more money on which to live.

**Longevity planning**—Health care, powers of attorney and medical instructions.

**Protection of assets from liability**—The family limited partnership.

**Divorce protection**—Keeping assets in the family.

**Special help for the family with an adult child who cannot handle finances**—How annuities work to provide a lifetime support without diminishing the legacy of siblings and grandchildren.

**Real estate**—Maximizing your real estate ownership for future wealth.

**How to talk to your parents and adult children about money—** Hurdling the final barrier to intimacy.

**Legal forms and clauses worth understanding**

## How to use this book

This is not a do-it-yourself book. It is a "know-it-yourself" book. The object is to understand the techniques used to build dynasties and legacies for generations to come. With a little planning, your family, too, will survive the asset drain that could defeat the spirit of education, free enterprise and hope for the future.

Not all of you will need all of the material in this book. Married couples will be attracted to different sections than singles. The 65-and-older set will find health care and estate-saving topics more interesting than those 40 to 65, who may want to focus more on legacy and estate building.

Still, I urge you to read *every* word of *every* section. The real purpose of this book is to show you ways in which planning and coordinating with other family members, spouses, siblings, parents and children, can make a real financial difference for everyone involved.

The ideas in this book are derived from my professional knowledge of the legal, insurance and brokerage industries. The presentation of material is based on my belief that anyone can understand complex tax material. So I haven't babied you. I have organized the material according to concepts and then put the practical application together for you. I don't want you to avoid lawyers, accountants and insurance agents. On the contrary, some concepts are so sophisticated that you won't be able to implement them without professional help.

But, I do want you to be able to meet these professionals on common ground, to never overpay, to get what you want and to avoid intimidation. Most of all, I want you to understand with precision what you are doing and its consequences for the future.

When I was a young lawyer I was told by a senior partner in the law firm where I worked, "All we produce here is paper." So true. But since the word processor was invented many lawyers buy computer programs for wills, trusts, living wills and more. They may not be able to explain the clauses they use or the practical future effect on your family and your money.

This book gives you the tools so that you can think for yourself. Read it all with confidence that you *can* understand it, and that you can, indeed, make your financial future—and that of your loved ones—what you want it to be.

# PART 1

## TRADITIONAL ESTATE PLANNING: DON'T BE A ONE TRICK PONY

Lately, people in the estate planning business have made their fortunes by selling a single, isolated concept—and selling it hard. Take probate avoidance, for example. Some experts have set themselves up as estate planning gurus by urging the avoidance of probate through the use of the revocable trust.

You'll learn all about probate avoidance, revocable trusts—and more—in this book. But, if you listened only to the teachings of the estate "healer dealers," you'd think that probate avoidance was a new thing, that they discovered it, and that every attorney is waiting in ambush for you to die so they can cash in on a probate proceeding.

The fact is that very few lawyers are in the field of trusts and estates. There are good reasons. First, the business of creating wills is, at best, a loss leader for them. People want to and should take time with their wills. Yet, a lawyer's fee for writing a will, no matter how complex, is a few hundred dollars at most. Next, most people want an attorney their age to help them with their estates. That means the lawyer will get business from their estate administration only if he or she outlives them—and is still actively working. Less than a fifty-fifty chance.

That's why estate planning was always the venue of the very rich. Their corporate law firms provided a special service for top executives to keep them from wandering to independent estate specialists. For this reason the traditional estate planning practice was based on the creation of trusts and wills, the appointing of executors and trustees, and the buying of insurance to pay taxes.

Probate avoidance and insurance coverage are not the only hot tickets around. Whole series of books are written on long-term care. Consultations on transferring your assets to qualify for Medicaid are all the rage—$400 per hour. Soon to come are promotions for suicide machines, chryonic burial (freezing), creditor-proof family partnerships and more.

Since this book will address most of these subjects—and since I am in favor of your having the consultation, buying the insurance and saving estate taxes and costs—what are my objections to the gurus in question? Just this: They create too *much* hysteria while generating too *little* information.

Imparting knowledge and guidance is the goal of this book—not whipping up the hysteria and hoopla connected with the more controversial estate planning issues. But to succeed in imparting such knowledge, I must first explain traditional fabrics of the estate plan: wills, trusts, taxes, gifts and competency. From these, all the fancy stuff stems.

In Part 1 you will learn about traditional estate practice so you can grasp and implement more exciting money-building and saving concepts presented later on. In my nationwide seminars, I am often confronted by worried and confused participants who've read or heard about just one aspect of estate planning and don't understand what to do. A catchy title may sell books (at least I hope it does), but one-idea presentations don't give you enough knowledge to set you on the road to successful estate planning. Avoid the one trick ponies and get the big picture.

# CHAPTER 1

# THE BIG PICTURE: WILLS

Wills are like teeth: Few people enjoy attending to them. They are, after all, a testament to our mortality, and it is much more fun to shop for new sporting equipment than to think about burial plots, probate, "wherefores" and "wherebys." In fact, people would rather spend a lot of money trying to avoid writing a will than a little money taking care of it.

All kinds of interesting devices—some that work, some that don't—have been set up to avoid wills. Many people put money into joint bank accounts with grandchildren and children just to avoid writing a will. That's dangerous. They don't realize that creditors and even spouses can make claim to the money while they still need it to cover their living expenses. Avoiding probate with joint accounts is one of the many warning signs of bad planning.

There are three basic reasons to have a will, and from each of them stem the other rules regarding estate planning. You can think of a will as the hub of a wheel, the spokes of which make up your all-round plan.

The three basic purposes of a will are: 1) to indicate *who* gets *what*—exactly the way you want; 2) to do your best tax planning; and 3) to pick the executors, trustees and other fiduciaries who are going to administer your estate. A healthy byproduct of will-making is that it forces you to learn a little about estate planning and requires that you put together a list of your assets so that you can begin to think about how you're holding money *right now*.

Your will is a document that should be tailored to your needs. It can provide for anything you please, so long as it is not illegal. Short of this, your will should reflect your wishes, covering your needs and your family's needs.

Will provisions are fairly standard in form, but that doesn't make them easy to read. Typically, they're expressed in "legalese." There are reasons for that. A will is one of the few documents for which I do not suggest the use of plain language understandable by lay people. The problem with plain talk is that while *you* may understand it, the judge may not. There are many time-honored phrases (we will look at them in a moment) that you must have in a will. These words have precise meaning to the courts, leaving no room for doubt. I have found that if you vary from these phrases, judges get confused, and lawsuits spring up. Remember, it will be the judge who will decide; you won't be around to help interpret. Spend the effort now to make clear to your lawyer what you want, then make him or her explain the language that will be used.

A will is only one document, but it takes the place of many more complex devices. If, after you have read about will clauses, you still don't want a will, you can do some things to substitute for one. Study this diagram of will substitutes.

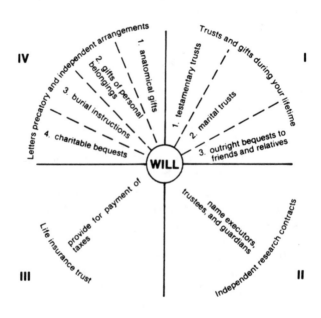

Section I of my "spoke diagram" shows that to leave your assets to particular beneficiaries you must give them gifts or make trusts during your lifetime.

Section II shows that you can research and interview prospective fiduciaries during your lifetime and enter into various contracts and agreements with them instead of having a will that names executors and trustees.

Section III helps if you want to provide for the payment of estate taxes, which you will have with or without a will. You can do this through insurance trusts, which pay the taxes for your estate as long as the premiums are kept up.

Finally, Section IV is useful if you wish to have special burial instructions or give your personal belongings to friends and relatives. You can do so by giving gifts or preparing a letter for your administrator. These are all will substitutes. But there is no one document that can accomplish as much in getting the right things to the right people as a will. It is true that probate can be expensive. But if you don't make a will, the government can end up choosing your beneficiaries for you.

## Concept 1

### What if you die without a will?

One good reason for having a will is to make sure that your money goes to the beneficiaries that you hold nearest and dearest—and not to those that the legislators in your state think most worthy. Every state has a statute determining which of your heirs will inherit from you if you die *intestate*— without a will. These heirs by statute are called your *distributees*.

For the most part, your representatives are filled with good intentions. They suspect that you wish your spouse to inherit the most, your children next, then your parents, and so on down the line. Still, there are always surprises on their list. The legislature of your state may make different decisions from those you would make if you were choosing. Further, if you move, the laws in your new state of residence will apply, and they may have an entirely different list of heirs for you! A will gives you the right to change the statute and impose *your* will upon the laws of inheritance.

Many people don't bother to make a will because they believe that all their money will automatically go to their spouses, or because they don't feel they have any heirs that they wish to protect. Even the many couples in our country who are living together but not married may believe that their money will go to the person they are living with. They don't realize that if they don't make a will, their assets may go to a sister or relative many times removed.

Here is a composite of many states to show you what could happen if you die without a will:

If only your spouse survives you, he or she will inherit everything, provided you had a valid marriage at the time of your death. If you are survived by a spouse and one child, the legislature has concocted the following distribution of property: First, a sum between $4,000 and $25,000 in money or personal property is given to the spouse. The remainder, if any, is divided between the spouse and surviving children. If you are survived by your spouse and grandchild, you will find that the same amount in money or personal property goes to the spouse, together with half of the estate; the other half will go to your grandchild. Most people, if they are survived by their spouse and a grandchild, would like all the money to go to the spouse, with perhaps a small sum to the grandchild.

If you are survived by your spouse and more than one child then your spouse gets the money and only one-third of the rest; the children divide the other two-thirds equally. If one of the children has died but had a child, that grandchild will take your child's share. If you're survived by your spouse, no children, and one or both parents, your spouse will get half, your parent(s) the other half. If any brothers and sisters survive you, all siblings will inherit equally. If one of them has died, his or her children will take their parent's share. If you are survived by your grandparents, they will inherit everything. Next, your estate goes to first cousins, first cousins once removed, and so forth. Your so-called "distributees" must be traced to a common grandparent.

While statutes provide for distributions to great-grand-parents, great-great-grandparents and their descendants, nothing is ever provided for someone you are living with, no matter for how long.

The point of all this is, of course, that you don't have to stand for it. You can make your own will and leave your property to whomever you please. Here is your big chance to do what you have wished you could do all along—what you know is right for you.

## Concept 2

### How to prepare to meet your maker— your *will* maker that is!

You'll save hundreds of dollars in legal fees if you are well-organized before you see an attorney.

Getting started is often the hardest part, so begin with this simple task. Write down who your beneficiaries are. To whom do you want to leave your money? Most of you know the answer and don't need help. Your spouse, children and grand-children—usually in that order.

### The spouse

Almost every state forces you to provide something for your spouse in a still-surviving marriage. In New Jersey, for example, you must give your surviving spouse at least one-third of your estate if there are any children. Most states let you leave it in trust; the inheritance need not be an outright gift. For example, in New York, if you want to leave money to a spouse in the most restricted way, you can leave a cash amount of $10,000 and place the rest of the one-third in trust for him or her.

A spouse—unlike children or grandchildren—cannot be disinherited. If you state in your will that you disinherit your spouse, that portion of your will is invalid. The spouse can elect to take his or her share even if disinherited. That's why this statutory share is called the spouse's "elective share." For more about this matter, read the concepts regarding divorce and remarriage later in this book.

## The children

After your spouse, consider your children. Are there any you want to favor? Are any minors? Do any have special needs?

Adopted children are no different from natural children and you don't have to treat them separately. If a will leaves property or money to "my children," the word "children" will be interpreted to include adopted children.

On the other hand, if you have "illegitimate" children—the law's word for a child born of parents who are not legally married and don't get married afterward—they will get nothing if you just use the word "child" or "children" in your will. To leave *them* something, you must specifically name them.

The rights of illegitimate children are still very skimpy. In many states, these children inherit from their mother's family, if there is no will, but not from their father's, unless there was a paternity suit first.

For the vindictive among you, do note that your children can easily be disinherited by a will, even if your spouse can't.

## The grandchildren

If your beneficiaries are children, you must think of *their* children, too. There are two phrases used in will "legalese" all the time that you should know. They are *per capita* and *per stirpes*.

*Per capita* means that you leave your money in such a way that it is distributed equally among those individuals of an equal degree of relation to you. The share of anyone who dies is divided up equally by the other beneficiaries of equal kinship. For example, your children, A, B, and C, are beneficiaries. If C dies, A and B divide C's share. If C had two children, C's kids get nothing.

*Per stirpes* means that if one beneficiary dies before you, the heirs of that beneficiary divide up the share. Literally, their heirs sit in their "stirrups" and inherit by right of their deceased ancestor.

In a per stirpes situation, your children, A, B, and C, are beneficiaries. If C dies, his share is divided between *his kids*, D and E, equally. A and B keep their original shares.

Do you want your money to go to your grandchildren equally, even though one of your children has had eight offspring and the others only one? Or do you want the grandchild with many brothers and sisters to receive less from you than the grandchild who is alone or has only one sibling? There is no right answer. Most people choose *per stirpes* so that the grandchildren get more if their parents have fewer children. Again, the only child wins out. Most grandparents believe that grandchildren should not get more than their parent would have gotten in the first place.

## The ancillary relatives

Next, think about the other people who are your heirs. To whom would you like to leave a lump sum? A friend? A sister or brother? A parent? A charity?

To help you finalize your thinking, look at the Financial Data Sheets in Appendix 4 and bring them with you when you see your lawyer.

---

### Concept 3

### How can I make a will if I don't know how much I'll have when I die?

Once you've gotten your beneficiaries straight, consider the amount you want to leave to each of them. Don't think that you must put specific amounts in a will. Usually you can't, since you don't know how to predict the future. Instead use percentages. Whether you have $5 million or only $5, you can still give 1 percent of your estate away.

Here are several ways you can leave your property:

**Bequest or Legacy:** A gift of personal property made in a will; a gift of real property made in a will.

**Legatee:** One who gets a gift of personal property in a will.

**Devisee:** One who gets a gift of real property in a will.

**Specific Bequest or Legacy:** A gift of an identified item.

**General Bequest or Legacy:** A gift that isn't specific, usually a sum of money.

**Demonstrative Bequest or Legacy:** A gift of property to be taken out of a larger holding of specific identified property.

**Residuary Bequest or Legacy:** A gift of the balance of all your property after payment of taxes, debts, expenses and specific, demonstrative, or general bequests or legacies.

---

## Things To Do

❑ Identify your beneficiaries.

❑ Determine if there is anyone you would like to disinherit.

❑ Determine what you want each beneficiary to inherit.

❑ Decide if there are special assets such as art or jewelry you want to give.

❑ Make a will and trusts file with all your notes.

❑ Make an appointment with a lawyer for two weeks from now.

---

### Concept 4

### Anatomy of a will and clauses for those making trusts, too

Since all wills have a similar format, let's dissect a standard will and study its anatomy. You'll find an example of an actual will in Appendix 2. It's annotated with questions to ask yourself and your attorney. We will examine a will, clause by clause, so you can learn the jargon and the meaning behind the words. I have highlighted with an asterisk those clauses that often appear in trusts that substitute for wills. You'll learn more about the probate-avoiding trusts later on.

## The revocation clause

Typically, wills begin simply enough with the statement that they revoke (replace) all other wills or *codicils* previously made. The usual language is:

> I, (your name) of (your address), do make, publish and declare this my Last Will and Testament, hereby revoking all former wills and codicils made by me.

In fact, this is so typical, many lawyers use preprinted fancy embossed stationery for it, and other lawyers have their word processors set up to type these words automatically.

Remember, you can make and revoke a will whenever you choose. I have one client who has made 16 wills in his lifetime...so far. Each subsequent will replaces the former—only the last one counts.

A *codicil* is an amendment to a will if there is some change you would like to see but don't want your attorney to remake the whole will. It saves time and paper, but that's all it saves. Most attorneys agree that you are better off having one will rather than a will and a codicil. Frequently, clients come into the office with a will and many codicils. If any of them were lost or misplaced, their wishes would not be followed. Limit yourself to one document, and use a codicil only in the event that you are going on a trip or are rushed and must get an amendment out quickly.

Even if you don't clarify revocation in your new will, subsequent wills revoke prior wills. But what if the second will is not valid? In some states, a person who makes a subsequent but invalid will ends up having no will at all. In other states, a prior will is revived (declared valid). This is why you read about heirs contesting the validity of existing wills, and coming up with old wills under which they have been named beneficiary.

If you have a will but feel it is inadequate and decide to make a new one after reading this book, make sure that your old will is properly destroyed. Tell your attorney to make a note for the file stating that you destroyed your old will. Then take the old will and throw it in the fire. Don't let that old will survive! In states where an invalid subsequent will does not revive an old will, the law of intestacy will apply. In other words, those old state laws will take over again. Be sure to make a new valid will.

## * Tax and debt clause

After you have told the world that you intend to revoke all your prior wills and codicils, you go on to assure the government that taxes will be paid, and your creditors that your debts will be paid. There are many ways to do this, depending on where you want the tax and debt payments to come from. Consider this example:

> I direct that my Executors (trustees) pay all my debts, including my funeral and administrative expenses and all estate, inheritance and similar taxes imposed by the government of the United States or by any other state or territory with respect to all the property that is required to be included in my gross estate whether the property passes under this Will or otherwise. Such expenses, debts and taxes shall be paid from (choice number 1) Residuary estate; (choice number 2) A portion from each beneficiary; (choice number 3) Paid from the bequest to (a stated heir).

Many attorneys will prepare this clause for you without discussion, but there are some significant points to consider. For example, your estate taxes can be paid right off the top of your gross estate or from the residuary portion (residue) of the estate. The "residue" of your estate is the property and money left after everything specifically mentioned is distributed. It usually goes to your major heir—the person most important and closest to you. If the taxes and debts are paid only from the residue, then your nearest and dearest will bear the full burden. If you have a few residuary beneficiaries, taxes will be prorated among them unless you say otherwise. For example, if one-third of the residue goes to charity and two-thirds to your spouse, there will be proportionate tax payments, unless you indicate to take it from the top first. If the taxes and debts are paid from the entire estate, then all the beneficiaries will be contributing. But you might have reasons for wanting one of the beneficiaries to pay everybody's taxes.

If you leave real estate to someone in your will and the real estate taxes were paid by the estate, the beneficiary of the property will have to reimburse the estate for those taxes. If you want the beneficiary who inherited the real estate to be free from taxes, say so; your fiduciaries (executors) will then pay the taxes from the rest of the estate.

This clause also directs the payment of debts such as your funeral expenses, perpetual care for your grave site, and any outstanding medical bills. Give some thought to the question of whom you wish to pay these expenses and put your decision into this tax and debt clause. If you are content to take the amount off the top of the estate at the beginning, you will be in good company, since this is the most usual way.

Avoid using the phrase "just debts," which appears in many wills. A debt may be *just*, but legally unenforceable; for example, a charitable contribution or a debt barred by the statute of limitations (the creditor waited too long to collect). Don't leave your executors guessing about this. You'll read more about debt clauses in a later section on solving special family problems.

## * Personal property clauses

The clause called the "specific legacy" clause is what most people think about when they think of making a will. This is the place where you give away specific items of tangible personal property to people. Specific stocks, bonds and other cash substitutes are also given here. This is the place to get a little sentimental and to be specific in regard to what you give away. Remember, the rest of the clauses will be very general, leaving pretty much whatever is left to the other heirs. Remember, too, that moving expenses, if any, are the responsibility of the legatee unless you say otherwise, and so are any liens against the property you leave. So if you really want to get even with your nephew who lives in Southern California, leave him the baby grand piano that you just bought on credit—which is now on the 42nd floor of your Manhattan apartment.

An example of a specific legacy clause is:

> I give the ruby ring known as the Kimmelman stone to my niece Sophie if she survives me.

Don't imagine that if you leave a specific piece of property, you are obligated to keep that property for the rest of your life. Many people who leave their gold earrings, say, think that they must change their will if they lose one of them, or if they decide to cash in because the price of gold has gone soaring. Not so. If you die without owning that specific piece of property, the legatee will simply not get anything. This is called ademption, or a "failed bequest."

What if you don't want the bequest to fail? You can state that in the event the personal property no longer exists, the legatee will get the dollar equivalent or another gift that you also describe.

A clear description of the item is critical in this part of the will. Many attorneys do not want to work out the descriptions for you. They call this the "pots and pans" part of estate planning. Make your description clear. Take a tip from Martha Washington, the childless mother of our country. Since she had so many wonderful possessions to give away, she drew little pictures on her will to make sure everyone knew exactly what she was talking about! You, too, should be specific.

## Letters precatory

Despite all this advice, there can be good reasons for leaving out specific bequests. Perhaps you do not want everyone to know who is to get your retirement watch or your engagement ring. The alternative to announcing the facts in a will is the "letter precatory"—a letter written in your own handwriting, signed by you and given to your executor. It can list all the odds and ends of personal property, both valuable and sentimental, without publishing who gets them in the will. The executor, of course, must be someone you trust to carry out your wishes. I suggest that you do list very valuable items in the will. For sentimental items, don't clutter up your will, just prepare a letter precatory.

Alternatively, the will can permit your executor, particularly if he or she is a spouse, to divide things up at his or her discretion. You could say for example:

> I leave my doll collection to my beloved daughters, and direct my husband, John, as executor, to divide them appropriately, having due regard for our daughters' preferences. John's decision shall be binding and conclusive.

To make life easy, you can leave your personal property in a general way. Try this:

> I give, devise and bequeath all of my jewelry, clothing, books, personal effects, household furnishings and equipment, automobiles and other tangible personal property, wherever situate, which I own at the time of my death, together with my insurance policies, to my children, share and share alike.

## * Money clauses

Next come the money clauses. Your will can give money and property to people in many ways. You can give a general legacy naming, a specific amount of money to be paid from the cash available in your estate. If there is not enough cash at the time of your death, then only a part of that legacy, or perhaps none, will be paid.

Rather than citing a specific amount of money—which may or may *not* be actually available when you die, you can express your wishes as percentages, giving one-third or one-half or some other fraction of your estate to your heirs. You can make the gift flexible. For example, you can leave "$50,000 or 5 percent of my estate, whichever is less." In this way, if you die rich, the legatee will get $50,000. If you wind up leaving a lot less than anyone expected, at least this beneficiary will get *something*...but your spouse or children or whomever will still get the *bulk* of your estate, as you intended.

There is even a type of legacy called the demonstrative bequest. This means that you give a certain amount of cash, and state where the cash is to be taken from. For example, you can give $10,000 out of a specific bank account. The beneficiary will not get the $10,000 unless the bank account itself is still in existence, even if there is $10,000 in the estate. In that case, specific and general bequests are paid first, *then* the demonstrative bequest is considered.

If you want to give stocks and bonds, pay attention to whether you are giving them as a specific or demonstrative bequest. If you want your beneficiary to get a particular stock that you own at the time you make your will, then name the stock and put down the certificate number right in the will. (You can still sell the stock, and if you do, that beneficiary will not get anything). Otherwise, if you just leave a general disposition of AT&T, then it's possible that your executors will actually have to go out and buy some of that stock in the open market at a time when you would not have recommended such a purchase. (Remember, if you do give a specific stock, it carries with it any stock splits that may occur after you have executed your will.)

No one can tell you whether to be specific or general in your bequests. But I can tell you which types of legacy will be paid first and which will fail if you don't have enough money to cover everything. Such failure is called abatement.

Legacies are paid in this order:

1. Gifts to a spouse that qualify for an estate tax deduction.
2. Specific legacies, if the item still exists.
3. Demonstrative legacies, if the fund they are taken from still exists.
4. General legacies.
5. Demonstrative legacies, if the fund specified does not exist, but other money is left.
6. Residuary gifts are paid last.

The order varies from state to state, and sometimes the legislature makes changes, but these guidelines are widely used.

## Trusts

Trusts are a separate and useful part of estate planning, and no anatomy of a will would be complete without reminding you that trusts, if you want them, can be set outright in your will. A trust allows you to name someone, a trustee, to manage a bequest for the beneficiary instead of the beneficiary getting the money outright. These kinds of trusts don't come into existence until you die and the will is probated. If you do create one, you can change it anytime you want, merely by changing your will. Several types of trusts are separately discussed in this book. Some can be drafted into a will are, such as credit shelters, QTIPS, generation-skipping and minor's trusts, and we'll discuss these in detail in later chapters.

## * The residuary clause

Everything that you have not given away in your specific bequests, that the government hasn't taken from you in taxes, and everything that you have not paid out to your attorneys, fiduciaries, doctors, and creditors, is called the *residue* of your estate. Since the bulk of your estate is likely to be involved here, the person or persons who generally inherit the residue of the estate are those who are closest and most important to you. They are called the *residuary legatees*, and the clause that gives them the remainder of your estate is called the *residuary clause.*

The words are fairly standard and very significant. They state that the testator (the person making the will—*you!*), leaves the "rest, residue and remainder of my estate wherever situated, whether real (meaning real estate) or personal (all personal property including stocks, bonds, bank accounts, etc.), to my residuary legatees." In other words, everything (including any specific bequest that has "failed").

You can leave this significant portion outright in trust for your family. You can give someone a specific bequest, like an automobile or a painting, and also make that person a residuary beneficiary.

## Burial instructions

You may include instructions for burial in a will, according to your needs and wishes. You should pay some attention to this subject. While it may be uncomfortable to think about, and may require a painful conversation, let your loved ones know what arrangements you've made and where the documents can be found. Sometimes giving them this peace of mind is the best legacy you can leave.

Most states have new statutes that cover anatomical gifts. If you want to give a portion of your body to science, say so in your will but *also* fill out donor cards. Call local hospitals for information. Once you're dead, speed is of the essence if your gift is to reach a needy recipient. There will be no time to do a real service for humanity if he or she has to wait for your will to be probated to get the gift.

## * Simultaneous death clauses

What happens if you and your beneficiary die at the same time, or examination can't determine who died first? Wills cover this, too, in simultaneous death clauses. Frequently, when beneficiaries plan their wills together these clauses crisscross, so that each one is considered to have survived the other. This means that whatever legacy you leave will go directly to your secondary choice of beneficiary. The same will happen to the person who died with you.

Many states have enacted the Uniform Simultaneous Death Act. In those states, the same result will occur if the will is silent on the point. The presumption is that each survived the other. This saves a double probate.

Here's what would happen if there were no simultaneous death clauses in the will, in a state without the Uniform Simultaneous Death Act: A brother and sister who died together in a crash had each made a will leaving everything to the other. Both named the same nephew, the son of another sibling, as their second beneficiary. If the brother was considered to have died *first*, the sister (even though already dead) would inherit, and an estate tax would be paid. The inheritance would then be paid out to her nephew, named in her will. It would be taxed again as part of *her* estate. By the time her nephew received it, two tax bites would have been extracted.

If the brother and sister have assigned a simultaneous death clause in each of their wills providing that, when in doubt as to who died first, the testator (the one who made the will) is presumed to have survived the other, this is what would happen:

| **Sister** | **Brother** |
|---|---|
| Brother gets nothing because sister is presumed to be the survivor. Only one estate tax is paid. | Sister gets nothing because brother is presumed to be the survivor. Only one estate tax is paid. |

**Nephew**

Inherits both estates, paying out
estate taxes on each *just once.*

Before including a simultaneous death clause, consider whom you want to inherit in such a situation. Let your attorney consider and explain the tax aspects.

## The *In Terrorem* clause

I have told you a lot about getting your property to the right people, but what if there are people to whom you *don't* wish to give anything at all? There is a will clause with the frightening name of *In Terrorem*. This is a clause that says, in no uncertain terms, that you do not intend to leave anything to the person named. In most states, you can disinherit your children. You might wish to disinherit one and not the other. Suppose that you have brothers and sisters, some of whom you want to help, others who don't need help or as far as you're concerned, don't deserve it. If there is any danger that people you want to exclude might contest the will, this is the time to use the *In Terrorem* clause.

It states that you have no intention of giving them (by name) anything and that if they should contest the will, the very fact that they caused trouble will result in their bequest failing.

## * Real property

Unless you specifically want to leave your real estate to a particular person, it is not necessary to have a special clause regarding it. It goes into the residuary and is left to the residuary legatee. However, some states require that at least the marital home (the home that the couple last lived in before one of the spouses died) be given to the other spouse. That right to real estate is called the *Right of Dower* when given to the wife and the *Right of Courtesy* when given to the husband.

What you *should* include in your will is the giving of a co-operative apartment. **A co-op is not real estate.** At least not as far as the law is concerned. Because it looks like shelter, many people would understandably, never believe this. When you own a co-op, you own shares in a corporation. The corporation owns real estate—not you. That means that you have to abide by the shareholder's agreement, usually embodied in the proprietary lease or in the bylaws of the shares to your spouse without interference by the board of directors. Some extend this to the rest of your family, others do not. Therefore, if you do own a co-op, check the bylaws and check the lease. A simple clause stating that you plan to give your shares to your spouse or next of kin will suffice.

## * Executors and trustees

The next part of your will generally names your trustees and executors. This is the individual(s) who will administer your estate and be responsible for the welfare of your kin. The clause itself is simple enough: for example, "I appoint my husband (or bank or daughter or family lawyer) to be the Executor (Executrix) of my will. If he (or she) fails to qualify or ceases to act, then I appoint my sister-in-law as the successor Executrix."

This is the portion of your will that demands those all-important decisions as to whether to have your major beneficiary act as the executor alone or together with a professional executor. In general, persons or banks or attorneys named as executors must post a bond securing their responsibility. But a will can (and most do) exonerate them from having to post that bond. What the testator *cannot* do is exonerate the executor from liability for failure to exercise due care. You wouldn't want to anyway—the whole idea is to have your fiduciaries be the most upright, forthright, and efficient persons you could find.

Guardians of a child can also be named in this clause. However, a surviving parent (even if the parents are divorced) can defeat the guardianship appointment.

## Signing the will

After a will is drawn, you generally come into a lawyer's office for what is called the will ceremony. This gives the lawyer the opportunity to tell bad jokes about estate planning and to have everyone sit uncomfortably in a forcibly light atmosphere: Lawyers call this "putting the client at ease." I suggest you make the visit to your lawyer more palatable by ending it with champagne. Bring a glass for the lawyer, too, especially if it's me.

The ceremony includes the attestation. You sign the will and state that you have read it, understood it, and attest that it is your will. This little ceremony is witnessed by two or three persons, depending on the state in which you sign the will.

The best witnesses are generally the secretaries or paralegal present in your lawyer's office when you sign the will. You can, of course, use virtually anyone, but relatives and friends are not the best choices. Even with the office staff as witnesses, you may have problems. After your death, it may be time-consuming and expensive, if not impossible, to bring together all of these strangers—who may have moved to opposite ends of the Earth—to swear that the will is yours. To avoid this, use a self proving will. To make your will self proving, simply use the witness affadavit in Appendix 2.

Even in the absence of a contest, witnessing is the kind of requirement that makes probate so expensive. Check with a lawyer to see if your particular state permits the special attestation clause, which avoids the need to bring in witnesses at the time of actual probate. An example of the clause is contained in Appendix 2.

---

# Things To Do

❑ Star the most important clauses to you as discussed in this chapter.
❑ Discuss them at the lawyer's meeting.
❑ Review any existing wills you may have.
❑ See how your will treats these important clauses.
❑ See Appendix 2 to be sure your will is self proving.
❑ See Appendix 2 for a sample of a short form and long form will. Study the annotations and note what you would like to discuss with your attorney.

---

# CHAPTER 2

# THE BIG PICTURE: TRUSTS

Trusts allow one person to put assets into the control of a second person in order for them to be used for the benefit of a third person. "Person" can be an individual, a bank, a corporation or other legal entity. A trust can offer many benefits:

1. **Professional management:** Entrusting others with the discretion to invest the assets because of their superior management skills ensures that your assets will be well-guarded.

2. **Tax savings #1:** Income tax is saved because a trust has its own tax bracket and rate, often lower that that of the person who transferred the assets.

3. **Tax savings #2:** If the trustee (the one managing the assets) distributes them to the beneficiary (the person the trust is aimed to support) and the beneficiary is in a lower tax bracket than the one who set up the trust (the *settlor*), income tax is saved as well.

4. **Tax savings #3:** If the assets are out of the ownership and control of the settlor, they won't be counted in his or her estate for estate tax purposes.

   **Warning: To enjoy any of these tax savings the trust must be *irrevocable*—once made it cannot be amended or taken back.**

5. **Avoiding probate:** Revocable and irrevocable trusts help avoid probate because the trustee can distribute the assets when you die and avoid probating

the will in surrogate's court. If the trust is revocable and you are the trustee, just name a successor trustee to take over immediately upon your death.

To set up a trust you must know your purpose, your trustee, and your beneficiary. The proper attorney to help you is a trust and estates lawyer. The clauses that you place in your will can also be in a trust. Some trusts are set up when you die. They are provided for in a will or in a living trust. Trusts that take effect only when you die are called *testamentary trusts*. Trusts that take effect during your lifetime are called *living* or *inter vivos trusts*.

Your estate executor or trustee will open the necessary trust accounts to implement your wishes regarding a testamentary trust. But, you must do the work to implement a living trust—especially if you plan to act as trustee, as is usually done in a trust designed to avoid probate.

You or your attorney's office will make a list of all the assets to be placed in the trust and change the name on the assets to "the trust of (name of beneficiary) on (date)."

Any asset, from homes to cars to cash, can be put in a trust. The trustee can be given the power to do anything legal with the money. You can be the recipient of the income of a trust with someone else getting the principal when you die or even before, if you so designate.

Trusts are truly the creation of the settlor. They may have many beneficiaries, trustees, and purposes. Throughout this book there will be many kinds of trusts discussed. All of you have heard of several of them. If there is one special type you are interested in, be patient, you'll read about it in one of these chapters. Before we look at the big picture, let's review the definitions:

**Trust:** a written document designed to put your money in the hands of a third party, so that the third party can use it *only* for the benefit of your designated loved one.

**Trustee:** the person to whom you give the money, so that he or she can handle it for your loved one.

**Beneficiary:** the loved one, the person you wish to get the benefit of the money.

**Corpus:** this is Latin for "body", but here it means the money itself or the bonds, stocks, diamonds or whatever else you wish to give to the trustee for the benefit of the beneficiary.

**Settlor or grantor:** you, the person who created the trust.

**Revocable trust:** a trust the settlor can revoke and stop.

**Irrevocable trust:** a trust the settlor cannot terminate; it goes on without control by the settlor once it has been made.

*Inter vivos* **trusts:** Also known as "living" trusts, these are trusts that you create during your lifetime. You can even be the trustee. The trust can terminate on your death or during your own lifetime. One that you create during your lifetime can pour over into another trust in your will so that it continues even after your death.

**Testamentary trusts:** These trusts are created in your will or in an *inter vivos* trust, and come into action only upon your death.

---

### Concept 5

### How *inter vivos* irrevocable trusts save you taxes

As with everything else in estate planning, remember that the government is interested only in taxing the estate for money in your control and possession at the time of your death. If you manage to take money out of your control and place it, instead, in the control of a trustee irrevocably, then upon your death the government will not tax the money. If, on the other hand, the trust is *revocable* (such as Totten or bank-account trusts where the money can be withdrawn at any time), then the government will tax whatever amount of money is in the trust.

So if it is estate taxes you wish to save, create an irrevocable *inter vivos* trust.

Many people believe that when they transfer assets and relinquish control over them by setting up an irrevocable trust during their lifetime, they are getting the total value of the assets transferred out of their estate. This is not true. We have a unified estate and gift tax. When you transfer assets to a trust, this is considered giving a gift to the beneficiaries of the trust. The assets will be taxed, either on April 15th of the year after you set up the trust, via the gift tax or at your death, through an estate tax calculation.

Later you will see that there are several exemptions from estate and gift tax. But presuming that none of the exemptions apply, the transfer itself will be taxed. The real savings from estate tax come because once the asset is transferred, its growth is no longer counted in the estate. For example, if Mary transfers stock worth $30,000 to a trust, that amount is taxable, assuming that none of the exemptions apply. But, if, at her death, the stock value has grown to $50,000, the extra $20,000 is out of her estate and never counted. That is why it is often best to transfer only appreciating assets to a trust if your purpose is estate tax savings.

Another benefit of an *inter vivos* irrevocable trust is that it can reduce income tax. A trust, like a corporation, is a new entity, separate from you—like a legal clone. That entity, not you, pays the income tax. The trust may be in a lower tax bracket than you are. This means that you may be taking money that ordinarily would be in a taxable savings account or other taxable investment and putting it in a trust, which is in a lower bracket.

Tax bites are measured by two things: first, the tax rate, and second, the tax bracket. The tax rate applicable to the taxable income of a trust is: 15 percent for annual income under $3,450, 28 percent for annual income between $3,450 and $10,350, and 31 percent for amounts over $10,350. This is higher than the tax rates for married persons filing separate returns, single individuals, heads of household or married persons filing joint returns—in other words, everybody!

However, if there is a mandatory payout of trust income to a beneficiary, the amount paid is deducted from the trust income and the distributed amount is taxed at the rate of the beneficiary. So if either the trust's or the beneficiaries' tax rate is less than yours, the income tax on the earnings is less.

More important, since the trust has only the amount of money you put in it, the trust's tax bracket will be lower than yours. Or the beneficiary's tax bracket may be far lower than yours.

Caution: To save income taxes the trust income cannot be used to support you or someone (such as a child) for whom you are legally responsible. Nor can it be used to fulfill your legal obligations (debts to creditors, for example), to pay your or your spouse's life insurance, or to be accumulated for you or your spouse.

You can save capital gains tax, too, when the *corpus* (what you put in the trust) is a highly appreciating asset. If you have rapidly appreciating stock, real estate, etc., that you want to sell, you can get some benefit by gifting it to a trust. Because you no longer own and control the asset, its appreciation (growth in value) is taxed at the trust's capital gains rate, not yours.

Gift taxes can be saved, too. To understand how, you must understand the concept of *present interest*—the right to use the assets transferred by the gift immediately. If I give you $5 to spend, that is an immediate gift. You have a present interest in it. If I give you $5 and say that you can spend it only when something happens—say, you get married—that's a "contingent," not a present gift. In fact, you may never get the gift if you never marry. If I give you $5 and tell you that I will keep any interest on the money, and that you will get the money only when I die, you have a contingent future interest.

The Internal Revenue Code has discount tables to be applied to the value of a gift that is not received until the death of the settlor. The tables are based on the age of the settlor at the time the gift was given and certain other factors. So, if you place $50,000 in a trust—income to you as a settlor for life then to the beneficiary of the remainder at your death—*less* than $50,000 is counted as the value of the gift. The discount tables are used to determine how to evaluate the gift for gift tax calculation. Since the gift is smaller than the actual amount transferred to the trust, the gift tax on it is smaller, too. You cannot get the discount by just giving the money outright, because that is a completed present interest gift.

Later, as we talk about special trusts that allow you to keep income for a period of years, the concept of present interest will become clearer and more practical.

### Concept 6

## Other benefits

Testamentary trusts and trusts created during your lifetime that do not terminate at your death, have lots of non-tax advantages, too. For example, there will be a continuity of investment handling. Even if you become unable to handle your money in old age, the person you name in the trust as your successor will take over—*not* someone appointed by the court. There will be a continuous flow of income to the beneficiary, and, of course, probate is avoided for the funds in the trust. A will leaving money to an heir who is already a beneficiary of a living trust can provide that the money left in the will be added to the *corpus* of the existing trust. There is no tax advantage, but continuity of management is preserved. This is particularly important if you expect a challenge by a person for whom you have not provided any inheritance.

Here is a comparison of what the *inter vivos* (living) and testamentary trusts can do:

### *Inter vivos* trusts

### *Testamentary* trusts

Saves estate and income taxes. Allows you to see how your fiduciaries control and use funds.

Controls the use of money even after death. Allows for long-range tax planning.

Takes effect during lifetime.

Takes effect at your death.

Gives property away irrevocably if estate taxes are to be saved.

Property remains yours during your lifetime.

Can be revocable; but no estate taxes will be saved.

Property is taxed along with the rest of your estate.

| | |
|---|---|
| Can save on income taxes because they will be paid either at the trust's rate or at the beneficiaries' rate. | No income tax advantage. |
| Allows you to designate a beneficiary of the income and a beneficiary of the principal when the income beneficiary dies. | Same. |

## Concept 7

### "Who's who" of trusts

Here is a "who's who" of trusts that you will find sprinkled throughout this book:

| Concept 8 |

# How trusts for children aid in money management

## Testamentary trusts for children

All wills and all probate-avoiding trusts should contain a provision if any of your heirs are minors. Your children may already be grown; but, if one predeceases you, perhaps their children will inherit. Parents of young children must always provide for a trust in the event that both die while the children are minors. Choose the trustee with care and think through the types of power and control you allow him or her to exercise. The trustee of the assets and the guardian of the child need not be the same people—but be sure they can cooperate.

On the other hand, if a surviving, estranged or divorced parent will become custodian by law, use a trustee who will care for the funds in the best interest of the child in the event the estranged parent is an unsuitable candidate. You can't control the custody of a natural parent, but you *can* use a trust to control the *money*. Give thought as to when you want a child's trust to terminate. It can be any age you choose. Most people distribute half the funds at age 25 and the rest at 35. Some distribute at the discretion of the trustee.

You can also terminate the trust during the lifetime of a grandchild and give the child money for life. See generation-skipping trusts later on in this concept, page 45, if you want to bypass your children altogether.

## *Inter vivos* trusts for the children

It can be very wise to create trusts for your children during your lifetime, because such trusts pack a three-punch wallop. First, they provide for the health and welfare of the children. Second, the trust income, if paid out and not needed for the direct support of the child, is taxed at the lower, child's rate. Third, any future increase in the value of the property belongs to the child, not the settlor, and, therefore, is out of the estate for estate tax purposes (if the trust is irrevocable).

You can give gifts to children in many ways other than trusts: 1) outright, putting the money or property in their names; 2) under the Uniform Gift to Minors Act; or 3) under custodianship arrangement. These all have their drawbacks.

For example, an outright gift belongs to the child when he or she reaches the age of 18 or 21, depending on the state in which you live. If the child should die, the money will go directly to the child's other parent, which may not be what you have in mind. Until a guardian is appointed, the gift will be frozen and cannot be used. To set up a guardianship entails a great deal of expensive legal red tape. The same is true for a custodianship arrangement, because, in some cases, you, the donor, cannot act as the custodian. If you do, the property is included in your estate should you die before your child. You'll learn more about the pros and cons of custodial accounts in the chapter on gifts.

## Special purposes

Trusts for children, both minors and adults, hold fascination for parents because they can solve certain family problems. For example, an incentive trust may be used for a child with a questionable future. The trust income can vary as the child's own earnings vary. Or if, for some reason, you dislike or distrust your child's spouse, you may use an incentive trust to provide for a different beneficiary of the principal upon your child's death. A child with a drug addiction can have an inheritance held—we'll learn more about that later.

## *The children of the children:* Generation-skipping trusts

For years the very rich have known what you are learning right now: That if you take money out of your control prior to your death, it is not taxable in your estate and can go to your beneficiaries tax free. But they wanted more. They wanted their money to descend through many generations without any estate tax. To accomplish this they created a trust, made a child the beneficiary during his lifetime, and provided that upon the child's death, the remainder of the trust would go to the grandchildren outright.

The trust rules permitted both income and principal to be distributed from time to time throughout the lifetime of the child. This meant that the trustees could make sure that the child had plenty of money to live on. When the child died, the trust money went to the grandchildren directly. Or the process could be prolonged, skipping from one generation to another. That is, the trust income could be distributed for the lifetime of the child, then the grandchild, then the great-grandchild, then the great-great-grandchild, and, finally, fall outright into the hands of the great-great-great-grandchild.

The result was that the money would not be taxed in the settlor's estate because it was not in the settlor's control at the time of death, and it would continue to pass through several generations and not be taxed, since none of the younger generations were in control at the time they died. Uncle Sam was being cheated out of taxes. So, in 1976, a generation-skipping tax was imposed.

This generation-skipping tax is imposed on trusts where there are two or more beneficiaries, at least two of which are from different generations, and where the settlor is a generation older than any of the beneficiaries. Typically, the generation-skipping tax affects settlors who are trusting money to their children and then to their grandchildren. These trusts can be made *inter vivos* or testamentary.

Trusts to your *children only* don't pay extra tax, trusts to your *grandchildren only* don't pay extra tax. Trusts to your spouse and then, upon your spouse's death, to your child don't pay extra tax (your spouse is considered in the same generation as you despite any actual age difference). Furthermore, even if you do have a real generation skip (your child and grandchild, for example) the first $250,000 is tax exempt altogether. This means that you must have a large trust *corpus* to worry at all about the tax.

If the beneficiaries are a child and grandchild, there is a $250,000 exclusion per child. So when the time comes to pay the tax, $250,000 is subtracted to get the taxable amount, but only if the younger generations are your children's heirs. Even then, the tax is imposed only if a transfer of the money or a termination of the right to get the money takes place. In the unlikely (but possible) event that the younger generation dies before the older generation, there will not be a taxable event at all.

The generation-skipping tax, when it is imposed, is an additional tax, separate from estate and gift taxes that may be assessed. The tax will be paid by the *trust*, based upon the estate of the "deemed transferor." That means that the child is deemed to have made the transfer to his or her own child, not the settlor to the grandchildren. This makes it almost impossible for your children to prepare their own tax picture accurately. By leaving money to their children, you may be interfering with *their* estate plan. If you are in this situation, consider creating separate trusts for each generation, rather than giving money for life to your own children and then to your grandchildren upon your children's death.

## Concept 9

### Choosing trustees

Whom should you appoint as trustee—a paid professional, an institution or a friend or family member? Each has advantages and disadvantages. The institution has the double advantage of continuity and personnel. It may have a large team of experts, so that if one expert leaves or dies, someone will be there to take over immediately.

The professional has the advantage of offering service, understanding and intimacy. A lawyer who knows the family and is sensitive as well as knowledgeable can make the investment suggestions best suited to individual cases. Remember, large institutions do not plan for you alone. They often have hundreds of other clients and make mass investment strategies.

The individual knows you personally and treats you specially. Frankly, individual experts may also be more in need of your business. They need you because you may make up 1 percent, instead of the one *millionth* of 1 percent, of their business.

Of course, there's a drawback. Individual trustees may discover problems they can't handle, and, therefore, have to hire other experts to help, using your money. Also, they may have no one to take over if they should become disabled.

Today, the practicalities of estate practice are such that no one can really handle it alone. Even those who appear to be individual estate planners work with accountants, pension planners, ERISA (Employee Retirement Income Security Act) specialists, even other lawyers to make your complete plan. When you talk to your lawyer, ask about his or her back-up staff.

## Double and triple fiduciaries

One solution that provides a broader range of expertise is the double and even triple fiduciary relationship. The major beneficiary is appointed as trustee together with an institution and an individual counselor. The counselor keeps up the dialogue with the institution and has equal say. The institution uses its expertise for investment.

Your individual lawyer can work immediately; there *is* no bureaucracy. He or she will listen to your wishes and react quickly. That doesn't mean you'll get your way; it just means you'll be able to voice your opinion and, as a fiduciary, have a vote.

Conflicts often occur between institutions and individuals. Perhaps I should say *especially* between institutions and individuals. To avoid this, get them together early. My clients have often sent me to lunch with a bank manager or trust officer of the institution they have chosen. That's very wise. We have a relationship and we work together. When something has happened to the institutional fiduciary, I have been there to educate whoever takes over. If something happened to me, the institution's professional would be there to educate my successor.

## Co-trustees

Using the co-trustee system may be the right way to involve both your spouse and a professional. You can give your spouse the right to fire the professional if the work is not being done properly, just as long as he or she appoints another one immediately. The problem with co-trustees is that although they are both equal fiduciaries, the spouse may feel intimidated by the powerful corporation that serves as co-trustee. He or she may be reluctant to participate. In response, the corporate trustee take over and make investment decisions without consultation.

The solution to this not-uncommon problem is to prepare your beneficiary. One good way is to have an open dialogue between your spouse and the institutional fiduciary. To help co-fiduciaries further along, have an emergency clause for illness or disability; a delegation clause for temporary absence; and a hold-harmless clause if one trustee (such as the shy spouse) doesn't participate. There can even be a difference-of-opinion clause in case there is an impasse. The language might read like this:

> In the event of a difference of opinion the (corporate) (individual) trustee's decision shall apply, provided it is given in writing to the other. The (corporate) (individual) trustee shall abide by the decision of the other and shall not be liable for the actions of the trustees made pursuant to the decision.

If you want to divide responsibility in a practical way, use the spouse or relative as a special trustee with review powers for paying out or distributing funds among beneficiaries (sprinkling), accumulating earnings rather than distributing them (accumulation), or dipping into principal to meet the needs of the beneficiary (invasion). In this way, the family member is making the decisions that affect the lifestyle of the beneficiary. For example, a sister can be named as trustee for the sole purpose of determining whether income should be accumulated or distributed among beneficiaries, the spouse, or even whether the principal should be invaded. An institution can have investment control.

Be flexible. Most things can be done. Just remember the criteria in judging fiduciaries: 1) *continuity*—will they be around long enough so that no one else has to stop and choose the fiduciary after you're gone? 2) *consistency*—is it an institution that changes personnel all the time? Is it an individual who passes you off to subordinates? 3) *conversation*—is there communication among you, your beneficiary and your fiduciary? (4) *calculation*—how have they done in the past with other people's money?

Once you decide on using a bank or other institution as your fiduciary, you take the next step—choosing a *specific* bank. How do you decide that a particular bank is right for you? Start with the people. How will the bank assign personnel to handle your account? The best institutions try to match customers to account executives and trust officers. Ideally, customers with similar needs will be served by a person who has expertise in the needed area. Ask about the procedure for switching within the bank if you're not satisfied. Don't be shy about this; it can and does happen.

Talk to the people at the institution, and have your spouse speak with them, too. Watch the kind of advertising and outreach they are doing with the public. Banks are not shy in disclosing the kind of business they want. It's up to you to express the kind of service *you* want.

Also, compare the investment policies at various banks and institutions. For example, do they use their own common funds as the vehicle for investing money in a trust for which they have been named as trustee? Ask to see performance records for three five-year periods. Compare these with the performance records of other common funds. Use the following indicators, which can be found in your newspaper, for comparison: Dow Jones Industrial Average, Standard & Poor's Composite Index, New York Stock Exchange Index. Ask what type of fund is being used. Is it one that emphasizes income, growth or tax-free returns?

Compare their requirements for accepting *you*. Most institutions will not take a trust and act as trustee unless there is a certain amount of money in the trust. Some banks are flexible. They may take a smaller trust if it is not complex and fits in easily with the kind of management they are used to.

See how institutions act with your individual co-trustees. For the most part, they will insist on being paid as much as they would be if they were sole trustees. Even more important is the relationship between the family member or individual lawyer named as trustee and the bank. Observe the dialogue that they set up with each other. This is particularly important if you have special assets to manage, such as copyrights and royalties.

If you are considering a bank and want to test the water, there are two ways of doing this before you name a permanent trustee. You can open an advisory account. The account is totally in your control, and no trust is set up. But the bank does give investment advice and handles your investments. The charge is slightly higher than for acting as trustee because it is not limited by statute. (In states without statutory limitations, the charges may be the same.) It is the investment advice in which you are interested. Familiarizing yourself with a bank's investment performance can be very important. A second method is to set up a revocable trust. This is a way to judge the performance of any trustee.

Finally, no trustee worth its salt will prevent you from including a discharge clause in your trust document. As you might want to change the trustee, it is also possible the trustee will wish to renounce its role during the course of the trust. Usually, however, if a trustee does not want to serve, it will simply not qualify at the time the *inter vivos* trust is created or the will is probated.

The expense of multiple trustees is not necessarily forbidding. Some states don't permit lawyers to double charge— they can't charge legal fees and fiduciary fees. Usually, legal fees are greater and prevail. Some states provide statutory limits for charges by fiduciaries based upon the principal in a trust each year. New York provides that three trustees must share the fee of two trustees if the trust is valued at between $100,000 and $200,000. If the trust is valued at more than $200,000, each trustee is entitled to one full statutory commission (unless there are more than three, in which case a total of three commissions is apportioned).

So you might pay the same amount as you would if you had only one institutional fiduciary and still need legal work. Banks and other institutions will provide rate schedules on demand, and require yearly minimum fees or they won't take the account. Look for lawyers on the staff. Question the fiduciaries about the complexity of assets they are used to handling. Pick an institution that operates in all of the localities where you have assets and beneficiaries. Ask your lawyer to advise you, and encourage coordination. Introduce your beneficiaries to the fiduciary, and consider their response.

In general, the thing *least* to be feared is that your money will be mishandled. People in this field are generally honest; if anything, they are overly conservative. As a fiduciary, your trustee must act with prudence, good judgment and reasonable care. If not, he or she can be accused of negligence or gross negligence. This can mean fines, loss of reputation or even imprisonment.

## Concept 10

### When can I act as my own trustee?

In deciding who should act as trustee of a living trust, your first inclination may be to consider yourself. Who better to handle your money than you? The fact is, you should act as your own trustee only for trusts created to avoid probate or manage money because these trusts are not used for tax savings. For the most part, acting as your own trustee will spoil your income and estate tax savings plans.

As long as you remain the trustee, you have not gotten rid of control over the assets, as Uncle Sam expects you to if you want estate tax shelter.

This means that neither you, nor those who may be under your control in the way they perform as trustees—your mother, father, kids, brothers, sisters, employees—can be named as trustee without your running into possible tax problems. There are, in fact, very specific things that a trustee who is the grantor himself, or someone controlled by him, cannot do without losing estate tax benefits. They include:

- You can't deal with trust property for less than adequate value. That is, you can't sell your trust assets to your own business for less than true value.
- You can't borrow without interest or security.
- You can't vote shares even in your own business held in the trust.
- You can't control investments.
- You can't substitute trust property.
- You can't allocate funds between income beneficiaries and beneficiaries of principal.

That's why it is fine to name yourself as trustee of a revocable trust that is created to avoid probate, but ineffective to name yourself as trustee of a irrevocable trust created to save taxes.

---

## Things To Do

❏ Think about trustees and executors.
❏ Ask your attorney for recommendations.
❏ Meet with bank officers who handle trusts.
❏ Get all fee schedules in writing.
❏ Ask about the investment philosophy of any trustee candidate..
❏ Ask your lawyer to send you a sample trust form for the type of trust you're interested in.
❏ Make a check mark on clauses you don't understand for discussion with your attorney.

---

# CHAPTER 3

# THE BIG PICTURE: GIFTS

When you give a gift, you save estate taxes because the government only taxes the assets in your control and ownership at the time of your death. As long as you've paid any applicable gift taxes on the gift, once its been given away, it can't be counted as part of your estate. But since the tax rate for estate taxes and gifts are the same, why bother? Because for tax purposes, the value of the gift is calculated at the time it is given, which can be a lot less than its value calculated at the date of death.

If you hold the asset and give it to your heirs in your will, it probably will have appreciated in value. So if you have heavily appreciating property that you do not need to live on, it is better to give it away *now* and pay the smaller gift tax. The growth in value of the gift is out of your estate.

## Concept 11
### The gift tax exclusion

The government permits you to give $10,000 per year per person as a gift without paying any gift tax at all and without including this amount in your eventual gross estate for estate tax purposes. This means that if you had five grandchildren you could give away $50,000 of your wealth every year as gifts and be free of paying any gift or estate taxes on that money. If you are married, you and your spouse can give $10,000 each, or $20,000 as a couple, to as many people as you want.

Before giving anything away, however, ask yourself some hard questions. How much do I really have to give away? Is there any chance I will need it? Would I be better off with a trust so that I can dictate the terms under which the money will be distributed? Deep down, do I expect anything in return other than tax savings, like loyalty or affection? Will a gift help my marriage? Will it equalize my spouse's financial position and mine? Do I want that? Yes? No? Why? Am I going to leave my spouse or children or whomever a lot of money? Would I like to test their performance now?

Don't feel guilty about facing up to these questions. If you're not honest with yourself, whom can you trust?

Having reviewed your resources, it is wise to make a gift-giving plan that takes advantage of the exclusion. If you have excess wealth that you know will eventually fall into your estate and be taxed, begin a program, say around age 50 or so, of divesting yourself of some of this money by giving it to your heirs on a yearly basis at a rate of $10,000 per year per donee. You can give it to as many donees as you wish—and they don't have to be relatives.

In addition to the $10,000 yearly per person exclusion, you pay no gift tax if you give medical or educational aid to someone for whom you are not legally obligated to provide, like a parent or your wife's child by a first marriage. However, the money for health or education must go directly to the institution, not to the friend or relative to pay the institution. This gift tax exclusion is unlimited and is separate from the usual $10,000 per year exclusion.

## Concept 12
### The Kiddie Tax

You can save income tax, too, by giving gifts. If you have assets that are producing income, you may want to give them away to someone who is in a lower income tax bracket than you. You are taking stocks, bonds, or other income-producing assets and giving them, let's say, to your minor children who are in a lower income tax bracket. They pay the income tax at their low rate and they own the asset and the income. Since you, as guardian, are in control of these assets anyway you really aren't losing much and you are saving taxes. But, beware of the Kiddie Tax.

Under the Internal Revenue Code rules, children under the age of 14 with income from investments are taxed at the same marginal tax rate as their parents. The first $1,100 is virtually tax exempt. After that, they are taxed at their parents' high rate. Form 8615 must be filled out along with the parent's own return..

If substantial gifts are given and parents' tax rates are high, use tax-free bonds or other tax-favored investments for children. After the age of 14, children are taxed at their own rate and can file a separate tax return. So, if you plan to make substantial transfers to children or grandchildren, check with your accountant first to be sure you are getting the income tax benefit you expect.

## Concept 13
### The Uniform Gifts to Minors Act

A statute enacted by every state is the Uniform Gifts to Minors Act. It is an alternative to giving gifts outright or in trust to persons under the age of 21.

To make such a gift, you can deliver the funds to a custodian for the donee. The custodian can be any adult member of the minor's family, a guardian, trust company, or a lawyer. But, if the gift is an unregistered security such as a bearer bond, the donor (you) cannot be the custodian. If the gift is of securities in registered form, money, life insurance policies, or annuity contracts, the donor can also be the custodian.

The custodian has very broad powers to hold, manage, or invest this property. His or her duties include the usual fiduciary responsibilities, such as registering the securities, placing the money in a specific account and keeping good records for inspection. The custodian can sell or exchange the property and use the proceeds for the minor.

All the money automatically goes to the minor when he or she is 21, becoming part of the child's gross estate. The gift once given belongs entirely to the minor and is irrevocable. While the custodian or donor controls and manages the money, the income earned on it is taxed only at the level of the trust, not at the level of the donor's income tax rate. Be aware, however, that if the donor names himself or herself as custodian and then dies before the minor reaches the age of 21, the value of the property will be included in the donor's estate for tax purposes.

Here are some pros and cons of how the Uniform Gifts to Minors Act works out as a tax saving device:

| PRO | CON |
|---|---|
| 1. The income from the investment is taxed at the lower income tax rate of the donee. | 1. The gift is irrevocable; once given in cannot be taken back. |
| 2. The use of money (and the income from it) can be controlled by the donor throughout the minority of the donee; this includes using it for the health and welfare of the donee. | 2. If the donee should die an early death, the money will be counted in his or her gross estate. |
| 3. The gift will automatically go to the donee at age 21. | 3. If the donor should die before the minor reaches 21, the money will be taxed in the donor's estate. |

## Concept 14

### Gifts of tuition

In response to the high cost of college tuition, many states have set up a college prepayment plan which allow a parent to prepay college even if the child will not be ready to attend for 10 years or more. A state-administered trust fund holds and invests the money until the child is ready to attend. All colleges insist that no matter what happens to their costs and charges by the time the child is ready to attend, his or her tuition will be considered paid in full. If the child goes to a non-state university or does not go to college at all, the money must be returned, minus a processing fee.

Unfortunately, the Internal Revenue Service has ruled that such payments do not qualify for the $10,000 gift tax exclusion because they are not present interests. Therefore, the payment requires an annual gift tax filing.

Further, the state is taxed on the income and growth of the funds. This affects the amount the state requires of the parent to reach paid up tuition.

Finally, if the child does not go to college, he or she is taxed on the difference between the payment made by the parent and the actual cost of college. I know of no other tax rule where a taxpayer is taxed on savings and not earnings. One would think that there is a concerted effort to keep the middle class out of college.

The taxation of these programs is in a state of flux and might improve or change, but make sure to check before taking any action.

## Concept 15

### Gifts to a spouse

Part of your gift-giving program can also include gifts to a spouse. Actuarial statistics tell us that the surviving spouse will usually be female. Therefore, most spousal gift-giving programs entail giving by the husband to the wife to divest property from his estate and place it in hers. The likelihood is that he will die first and the wealth will be taxed only once, upon her death. Gift giving to a spouse is encouraged by the federal government. Interspousal gifts may be unlimited, and no gift tax is paid, no matter how much is transferred back and forth. This is similar to the unlimited marital deduction available to you for gifts given in wills. Gifts given to a spouse prior to Jan. 1, 1982, go by the old rules, which were much more limited. Formerly, you could give $100,000 during your lifetime to your spouse without paying a gift tax and without its being included later in your gross estate for estate tax purposes. For gifts over $100,000, a gift tax was imposed and couples had to be aware of the tax implications. Today you need not make such gift tax calculations.

When we discuss the *Superclause* in Chapter 7, you will see that this method of dividing assets between spouses in a special way can save up to $192,500 in taxes. It is because no tax is imposed on intra-spousal transfers that the Superclause can work.

## Concept 16

### Gifts *causa mortis*

Gifts *causa mortis* (in contemplation of death) are treated as any other gift. The $10,000 exclusion and unlimited spousal exclusion applies. This is recent, too. Prior to Jan. 1, 1982, a gift given within the three years prior to death was counted in calculating estate or gift taxes—only the exclusion (then only $3,000) applied. The government presumed that you were giving money away in old age to avoid estate taxes.

The one exception is for gifts of life insurance. A policy's death benefit is counted in the estate for tax purposes if it was gifted within three years before the donor dies. You'll learn more about this when we fashion *Dynasty trusts* in Chapter 9.

## Concept 17

### Stepped-up basis

If you do plan to give gifts very late in life, or to wait until you are very ill, you should consider the issue of capital gains. Here is the dilemma: If you give a gift of appreciated property during your lifetime, the recipient takes it with the same basis that you had. This means that when the recipient sells it, the gain will be reckoned as the difference between the sale price and your original purchase price.

On the other hand, if you leave the property in a will, it is transferred on a stepped-up basis; that is, its value is judged by its worth at the time you die or six months later (executor's choice). When resold by the beneficiary, the gain is less, and, consequently, so is the capital gains tax. You must decide whether the extra estate tax paid by giving appreciated property as an inheritance instead of during your lifetime is more or less than the capital gains tax saved by making a testamentary gift. There is more about this in our real estate section.

## Concept 18
### Gift tax filing

You need not file a gift tax if your gift is under $10,000 per beneficiary per year, a gift between spouses, a gift of a future interest, a gift directly for medical or tuition expenses to the provider of the service paid by one not legally responsible for the beneficiaries' support.

If you give a split gift of $20,000 per beneficiary as a married couple, you must file form 709—a simplified form—but you will pay no tax.

Otherwise, all gift givers must file form 709 on tax day. (You can get an extension, just as you can for filing all the rest of your tax forms.)

You can opt to pay no tax, but to apply the unified credit to the amount you owe. You will learn a great deal more about this in Chapter 5.

## Concept 19
### Joint ownership

There are many types of gifts we might make every day without really thinking about it. Here are some, and their consequences:

- Opening a joint bank account in your name together with either a child or an adult: No gift is made and no tax incurred until the other person makes a withdrawal. If you both contributed equally, there is no tax.

- Putting two names on United States bonds: A tax is imposed when the other person cashes in the bonds. If you cash them and keep the money, there is no gift tax.

- Buying joint stock: A gift is made as soon as you designate another as joint owner.
- Placing someone else's name on real estate: A gift is made when the new deed is executed.

Remember that no tax is imposed for transfers between spouses. This applies to the above "everyday" type of gift as well.

What happens when one joint owner dies? If the joint owners are husband and wife, one-half of the property is counted in the decedent's estate for estate tax purposes. The surviving spouse will automatically inherit the property unless a different designation is made. If the joint owners are not husband and wife, the amount of the property included in the decedent's estate is based upon who purchased and contributed to the property. It is possible for 100 percent of its value to be included.

---

## Things To Do

❑ Wait to be certain that you have a taxable estate.

❑ Determine if you can spare assets to give gifts.

❑ Note your beneficiaries.

❑ Be honest about contingency gifts (attach strings if that's what you want).

❑ Begin a gift-giving program only after you have exhausted other avenues of tax phasing.

❑ Before giving directly to adult children, consider the Dynasty/Legacy approach in Part 2.

---

# CHAPTER 4

# THE BIG PICTURE: PROBATE

Everybody wants to avoid probate...despite the fact that few people actually know what it is—or *why* they want to avoid it. Probate is a legal proceeding required to validate a will. If you have a will, no money is distributed until the will is probated.

Probate takes place in the state court, in the state where a person resides at the time of death. These courts are often called *widows' and orphans'* courts, or *chancery* courts. A fancy name is the *surrogate's* court. ("Surrogate" is another word for substitute; the idea is that the judge in these courts is a substitute for the deceased.) If there is any question as to what the deceased meant in his or her will or intended at the time of death, the surrogate or substitute (the judge) will decide.

The legal set-up is similar in all states. The executor named in the will files it and a probate petition with the surrogate. The surrogate, after determining that the will is genuine and valid in its form, accepts it for probate and orders that legatees (those you left money to) and distributees (those that would inherit by statute if you had no will) are notified, so they can present claims against the estate, if there are any. Sometimes you see such notices in local newspapers.

This is the time when heirs who are disinherited get into the act to try to set aside the will. Once all the assets are before the court, and either no claims by disappointed heirs have been made or claims have been settled and the fees of administration have been paid, the probate is complete. At this time, I.R.S. forms are presented separately and taxes paid.

You have two choices. You can do everything necessary to avoid probate (this takes work, planning and money) or you can do everything to take advantage of what probate has to offer and minimize its bad effects (this, too, takes work, planning, and money). What you can do, for free, is understand probate enough to make the right choice for you. First, you need to forget some myths.

## Concept 20
### Myths about probate

**Myth:** *If you avoid probate, you save taxes.* On a true-false test, the answer is false. Probate has nothing whatever to do with taxation. Taxes are based entirely upon the assets that people have in their control when they die. If money is in your control, the government is going to find a way to tax it. A good deal of this book helps you take money out of your control for tax purposes and still be able to use it efficiently for the purposes that you choose. If you avoid probate entirely, you will still be taxed under the same rules and in the same amount as if your estate was probated.

**Myth:** *If you have no will, you won't go through probate.* False again. If you have no will, then the court must appoint an administrator (since there is no executor named in a will). That alone requires a member of your family to go to the probate court to be designated as administrator.

**Myth:** *Probate takes place in only one state.* Residence is the key to probate. The problem is that in our mobile society, people often reside in more than one place. The older couple who keep their condominium in Florida and a vacation home in Connecticut can have double trouble when it comes to probate. Where do they reside? There was a time when multiple residences were for the rich. Today, just because housing is so expensive, many people put their estate dollars in a small country place in another state and pay rent in their main state of residence. The court will look to where the deceased voted, kept property, kept bank accounts, worked and had friends to determine residence. The residence you list in your will is not binding on the court.

### *Dying May Be Hazardous to Your Wealth*

**Myth:** *It is cheaper to have a family member as executor rather than a professional, i.e., an attorney, banker, accountant, etc.* This is the kind of true-false question that you used to hate because the best answer is maybe. A professional, of course, will charge a fee. Your relative will not charge a fee, and your will can even state that the executor shall serve without a fee. But "fee-less" or not, the family-member executor must know what he or she is doing or it will be necessary to hire an attorney to help every step of the way. Professionals may charge on an hourly basis or ask for a percentage of the estate. Either way, they may earn at least what they would have earned had they been named in the will. So the simple answer is either to obtain professional help or have a knowledgeable family-named executor. A knowledgeable executor can work with an attorney to minimize costs and not be at the mercy of the professional's superior knowledge.

**Myth:** *While probate is proceeding, no money can be distributed from the estate.* False again, luckily for you and your beneficiaries. A good executor (one with a heart and a head) knows the needs of the beneficiaries and makes every effort to distribute the funds as probate goes along, particularly if the probate proceeding will take a long time. Probate can be lengthy—often annoyingly so, sometimes hair-raisingly so.

Rather than letting your beneficiaries go begging to an executor, make sure your beneficiary has sufficient funds to live on as soon as death occurs.

Do this by purchasing an insurance policy payable directly to your beneficiary. Such policies do not go through probate, even if you do have a will and even if the estate itself is going through probate. One of my good friends and one of the best insurance agents in the world suggests that the first person a beneficiary should call upon the death of a family member is his or her agent. It's not a bad idea. It's also a great idea to give a simple power of attorney to your beneficiary to permit him or her to withdraw funds from your account while you are ill; it will avoid disturbing you in a sickbed in order to take money from the bank. Insurance policies, power of attorney, and a wise choice of executors all permit money to be collected even while probate is going on and even while an estate is being "tied up."

**Myth:** *If I put everything in joint names, I can avoid probate.* False. Joint ownership has pitfalls you'll probably want to avoid even more than probate! For example, if a divorce or bankruptcy occurs with one joint owner, the entire account can be in jeopardy.

There are many kinds of joint ownership. *Ownership with right of survivorship* means that the survivor will automatically inherit, which does avoid probate. But not all joint ownerships have the right of survivorship; most, in fact, do not. In general, regardless of what state we are talking of, if property, real estate, stocks, bonds, and most other assets are held jointly and there are no special provisions for right of survivorship, they are not owned that way.

Another type of joint ownership is called *tenancy in common* and has no right of survivorship. The deceased's half must be probated and will be left to his or her next of kin according to the rules of intestacy. No probate has been avoided.

Even if you do carefully use the magic words "right of survivorship," a problem arises if there is a common disaster and both you and your joint owner die simultaneously. Once again, *who* takes *what* must be probated.

Problems also occur if a joint owner becomes institutionalized. The wife that outlives her husband for years but who becomes mentally incompetent soon after his death may end up being the owner without probate but is really incapable of using and preserving the money. What happens? A friend or relative usually applies for a conservatorship to conserve the assets. Where is this application made? Back in the probate or surrogate's court.

So if you do want to avoid probate by joint ownership, make sure that you use the words "right of survivorship" wherever they are required and hope that your co-owner survives you—in good shape and good health.

**Myth:** *There is a magic, foolproof, painless formula to avoid probate.* Yes, and there is also an Easter Bunny, Santa Claus, and Tooth Fairy. What has been suggested as a method of avoiding probate altogether is the *inter vivos* trust—also called a revocable or living trust.

## Concept 21
### Revocable, Probate-avoiding trust

You can avoid probate entirely by taking every type of property that you own and transferring it to a trust naming yourself as trustee and beneficiary while you are alive. Name one of your loved ones as beneficiary and trustee when you die.

Here is an example: You own a home and other assets and wish to have your sister inherit it all after your death. You have no spouse and no will. You would like to avoid making a will so that no probate takes place. You want to make sure your sister gets the property. What can you do? You set up a trust naming yourself beneficiary during your lifetime and your sister as beneficiary when you die. Give yourself control over the property for your own lifetime by naming yourself trustee. Name your sister successor trustee. She will take over immediately upon your death and will have the power to deed the house and other assets over to the beneficiaries (herself). No court order is needed. Leave this trust document with your important papers. Since there is no question that the property will go to your sister, no will is needed to leave the property to her and, therefore, you avoid probate.

## Concept 22
### What's the downside of the probate-avoiding trust?

1. To truly avoid probate you must have trusts that cover all your property, including stocks, bonds, bank accounts, real estate and anything else you may own. The preparation of the trusts, unless you really expect to do everything yourself, is more expensive than the preparation of a will.

2. Unless you dispose of each piece of property, you will need a will anyway. Hence, the expenses of preparing a will and of a smaller probate proceeding can't be avoided unless you diligently place the property in trust every single time you get new property.

3. Since life, I hope, is dynamic and you are constantly buying and selling, owning and giving up types of property, you must be on top of these changes. On pages 68 and 149, you will read about the Springing Power of Attorney, which will help make the job of avoiding probate simpler.

4. And despite what some anti-probate enthusiasts imply, no taxes are saved by making revocable trusts during your lifetime. Again, do not confuse the avoidance of probate with the avoidance of taxes. One has nothing to do with the other. If that is all you learn from these pages, that would be good enough. Taxes refer to the money the government wants after your death; probate refers to the procedure for determining who your heirs are after you die. That procedure can be expensive and lengthy, and all schemes to avoid probate are to avoid that *process*—not to avoid taxes.

## Concept 23

### Avoid probate if:

1. Your state has very complex laws.
2. Your estate has complicated assets.
3. You have assets in more than one state.
4. Your heirs lack competency or inclination to deal with business matters.
5. You want privacy.
6. You do not mind spending your own time and money now to save your heirs' time and money later.

## Concept 24

### What to do if you decide to avoid probate

See a lawyer. This is not a do-it-yourself project no matter what the pop culture, law-for-laymen books say. Use the revocable trust as a catalyst to plan for tax savings and for longevity. Read the chapters in this book on powers of attorney and note that you can spell out what you wish to happen if you cannot act as trustee because of illness.

Also, use the trust to do some real tax planning. In itself, the trust saves no taxes, because you do not relinquish your control over trust assets. But a revocable trust can provide for a *credit shelter trust*, which I call a Superclause. This applies only to married couples and is dealt with in Chapter 7.

Finally, make sure that all your assets are in the name of the trust, not *your* name. Any assets outside of the trust will not avoid probate or administration. If you use a Superclause, the assets also have to be divided up between spouses in the correct manner. Use your attorney to coordinate these efforts.

You can even set up a probate-avoiding trust and leave it unfunded. You will need a special power of attorney called a *springing power*, discussed on page 149.

---

## Things To Do

Ask yourself whether:

❏ Your assets are complex.
❏ You have heirs in other states or countries.
❏ You have property in other states or countries.
❏ Your heirs have good business sense.
❏ You don't mind handling your estate; paying more now to save money and trouble for the family later.
❏ Your state has complex probate statues.
❏ If you answered yes to the above questions, you should avoid probate.

---

# PART 2

## ESTATE TAXES: A NEW PROBLEM FOR THE AMERICAN MIDDLE CLASS

Our nation was nearly 150 years old before an estate tax law was enacted. Before that, any amount of assets could be accumulated and passed on through the generations. The early 20th-century robber barons, among others, were thus able to create dynasties through their fortunes without giving much back to the public.

The political history of the estate tax was fraught with controversy, intrigue and bribery. But even the shrewd and successful American industrialists could not foresee the effect of the tax. To our benefit, it put a brake on the runaway accumulation of riches by a few. To our detriment, it penalizes the center core of middle-class Americans, a group into which *you* most likely fall.

At least one-third of all your estate planning will be devoted to the pursuit of tax savings. It is an area where a small expenditure for professional help can save thousands of dollars, making it the most cost-effective part of your plan.

# CHAPTER 5

# HOW MUCH ESTATE TAX WILL YOU PAY?

Anywhere from 0 percent to 82 percent of your estate will wind up disappearing into Uncle Sam's pockets, depending on the size of your estate and the plan you have made. It is possible that two estates of the same size can be taxed quite differently—one estate suffering devastating tax damages and the other surviving with minimal losses—if tax planning was absent in one and diligent in the other.

You will understand why the field of tax planning is so fertile as we review each concept.

## Concept 25

### How large is the estate tax?

The estate tax table found in Appendix 5 shows that the tax starts at 37 percent on the dollar and climbs to 55 percent for estates of more than $3 million. *State* estate tax is over and above that amount. It varies from state to state and can be as high as an additional 27 percent. Usually, when you do federal tax planning, you are doing your state tax planning as well.

The good news is that before the tax tables are used, there is an exemption from any taxation of $600,000 per person. This exemption was part of the Reagan administration tax reform, and can be changed by Congress. The law was enacted in 1981 and is already under attack. For now, however, all planning assumes that the first $600,000 of your estate is tax free.

If your assets are less than that (use the form in Appendix 6 to calculate them), you may not need planning. But don't count on it. Assets grow. By the time of your death, you may have accumulated a taxable estate. It is reported by Metropolitan Life, using in part surveys done by Life Insurance Marketing Research Association (LIMRA), that the shrinkage of an estate counting taxes and expenses is:

20%—$500,000
30%—$800,000
33%—$1,000,000
38%—$1,500,000
42%—$2,000,000
48%—$5,000,000

These figures are based on the estate of a couple who've done some minimal planning. So, before you dismiss this part on estate taxes as unimportant to you, recalculate your assets taking into account their growth at a very conservative 5 percent a year until your death. Assume an actuarial date of death as 74 for males and 84 for females. If you are still convinced that your estate will never exceed $600,000, skip to the next Part. But, if you determine that your estate already exceeds $600,000 or it most likely will in the future, use Appendix 5 (the tax table) to see how much of your hard-earned money may go to Uncle Sam if you don't take the time to do some serious planning...right now.

Remember, too, that the estate and gift tax tables are the same. As you know, $10,000 per year per beneficiary can be given with no gift tax ($20,000 if the couple gives the gift). Beyond this amount, a gift tax is imposed.

For example, you give $12,000 to your son, you and your spouse give $24,000 to your daughter, and you give $25,000 to your church. Your gift tax, then, is based on a gift of $6,000. Here is why: The first $10,000 of the $12,000 gift to your son is tax free ($2,000 is taxed), the first $20,000 to your daughter is tax free because it was given by the couple ($4,000 is taxed), the gift to charity is always tax free no matter how large. As you can see, when couples write a check on a joint account rather than on an individual account, they have doubled the excluded amount from gift tax. That's how simple the plan can be.

Even if the gift is taxable, you can choose not to pay the tax. You can file a gift tax return and elect to debit your $600,000 exclusion.

## Concept 26

### What are some ways to save taxes?

A good way to find out what you can do to save taxes is to review the way estate taxes are calculated. As you do, the strategy best for you will become clear. Here is how to calculate your estate taxes:

### The gross estate

The gross estate includes the value of everything you own at the date of your death. This includes joint assets. If owned as husband and wife, one-half of the value is included; if not owned as husband and wife, 100 percent of the value of joint assets is included in the gross estate of the first to die. To avoid this, it must be shown that the survivor contributed to the fund. Insurance policies still owned by you, powers of appointment, rights to royalties, copyrights and other exotic assets are counted as part of your gross estate as well. Your real estate, stocks, bonds and cash are also counted.

Additionally, money you control, such as assets in a probate-avoiding revocable trust is counted.

Adding up all your assets should give you your first idea of how to save estate taxes—just reduce the amount counted in your gross estate. But, if you do that, you will obviously relinquish ownership and control of your assets. In some cases, where there is money to spare, you can do just that through a gift-giving program to children and grandchildren. You learned about this in Part 1. Shortly we will see how you can make such gifts and still keep a limited right to use the money yourself.

## Expenses

From the gross estate, deduct the final expenses such as doctor bills, attorneys fees, funeral costs and debts the estate must pay. LIMRA estimates the average final expenses nationwide, not counting professional and executor's fees, as $19,000.

Therefore, to save taxes, if you are a fiduciary, keep track of everything from phone expenses to transportation to the funeral, and pay it from the estate.

## Adjusted gross estate

The gross estate minus these expenses is called the *adjusted gross estate*. From this figure any charitable donations are deducted—dollar for dollar. In a subsequent Concept (see page 21), single taxpayers can learn how to combine the charitable deduction with a life insurance policy to save taxes for their children and grandchildren.

The marital deduction is also taken from the adjusted gross estate. There is a so-called unlimited marital deduction. One can leave any amount of money to a surviving spouse and *all* of it will be deducted. If your will or trust leaves everything to your spouse, then the adjusted gross estate is reduced to zero. That's why many loving couples have no tax when the first one dies. However, a tax may be imposed when the second one dies. In Chapter 1, you learned how the use of a *Superclause* in a will or trust can also reduce taxes in the second estate.

A third deduction from the adjusted gross estate is derived from a stock redemption plan. Often, if there is a family business that is incorporated, the shareholder's agreement provides that stock in the family business held by a shareholder at the date of his or her death will be redeemed (repurchased) by the corporation. The purpose is to give the widow or widower cash and to keep the stock from getting out of the ownership and control of the surviving family members working in the business. The effect of this on your taxes must be discussed with your accountant or business attorney.

It is now clear that there is another way to save taxes: Take advantage of marital and charitable contributions.

## Adjusted taxable estate

To the adjusted gross estate (minus these deductions) you must next *add* the amount of non-excluded gifts you gave over the years. Any gifts over $10,000 per beneficiary per year ($20,000 if given by a couple) after 1981, and over $3,000 if the gift was given before 1981, must be added back to the adjusted gross estate. That is why gift giving does not actually remove the gifted amount from tax. It only removes the growth on that gift which would have accumulated through the years if the money was not given away.

Take the figure derived from the adjusted gross estate plus gifts given and look up the tax on the tax table. See Appendix 5. This is the tentative estate tax due.

## Final tax

From the tentative tax, deduct any gift taxes paid during the course of the decedent's life. Also deduct any foreign tax, or other credits. Finally, deduct a sum of $192,800. Why? This is the amount of tax on $600,000 of estate value. When we actually calculate our taxes, the credit is applied to reduce the tentative tax. For example, if the tax on the adjusted tax estate is $500,000, reduce it by gift tax paid, foreign estate taxes paid *and* $192,800. (The $600,000 exclusion figure is just as handy to do quick calculations to see if our estate is large enough to be taxable in the first place.)

# CHAPTER 6

# BUILD FAMILY TRUSTS TO REDUCE ESTATE TAXES

The single easiest way to save taxes is to reduce your gross estate. Be poor when you die. Transferring all your assets—moderate gift-giving programs for children, grandchildren and others as well as charitable giving—works. Except that you will have nothing to live on!

I strongly recommend against giving money away on a verbal understanding that you will get the benefit of it. Divorce, debt and change of heart can occur in the life of the person to whom you gave the money.

You already know a great deal about gift giving and setting up irrevocable trusts. All these reduce your estate by at least the growth in value of the assets transferred. But they also deplete you of the money you may need for income. There is a group of trusts, usually with family members as beneficiaries, that allow you to "have your cake and eat it." All you need is a grasp of the concept of "present interest." Turn to page 41 and review that concept before you read on.

## Concept 27
### GRITS: Grantor-retained interest trust

The GRIT is a trust in which you, the grantor, transfer property for a period of time. The trust is irrevocable once signed. During the period designated in the trust, the grantor gets income. When the period is over, the trust terminates and the beneficiary receives the principal. No tax is paid at that time.

When the trust is made, the amount transferred is a gift. The normal rules apply. If the amount transferred is less than $10,000 per beneficiary of the trust, then no tax is paid. If it is more, the grantor can pay a gift tax or elect to defer the payment as part of the estate tax plan.

If the grantor outlives the period designated in the GRIT, all is well. The amount in the trust is not counted in his or her estate. None of the growth is counted. And, even though the grantor used the income from the trust, he or she is not considered to own or control the assets.

However, if the grantor dies before the term of the trust expires, all the assets in the trust at the time of death are counted in his or her estate. Motto: Outlive the period designated in the GRIT. Don't have your cake and eat it for *too* long.

GRITS are used specifically for real estate as an income-producing asset.

## Concept 28
### GRATS: Grantor-retained annuity trust

A GRAT is essentially the same as a GRIT. It differs only in that the grantor must receive a specified fixed percentage of the value of the property in the trust for the period of years. The GRAT is not limited to real estate. If the grantor survives the income period the total trust fund is excluded from his estate. If he dies prior to the expiration of the period, an amount necessary to annuitize (pay out) the percentage for the remainder of the period is counted in his estate. This is the amount he would have received if he lived for the full period. Therefore the Internal Revenue Code deems that amount an asset of the grantor upon death.

## Concept 29
### GRUTS: Grantor unit trust

The GRUT is the same as the GRAT except that the income stream is not the same percentage each year. Every year the percentage is reevaluated. GRUTS are useful to those who want flexibility in the amount of income they receive each year.

| Concept 30 |

## GRITS, GRATS, GRUTS: An overview

All three are irrevocable trusts made to get rid of assets from your gross estate while you retain some rights to keep the interest income from the investment of the money for a period of years. Usually when you transfer assets to an irrevocable trust with the beneficiaries getting the use of the income—such as a child's college fund trust—the amount you transfer to the trust each year over the gift tax exclusion is counted in your estate when calculating the final tax.

For example, if you set up a trust with $15,000 for a two-year-old, the amount counted in your estate is $5,000. The first $10,000 is excluded under the gift tax exclusion rule. And all of the growth through the years on the *entire* amount is also excluded because you gave up control over the asset.

When you set up a GRIT, GRAT or GRUT, there is an even greater exclusion. Because you have a right to get some of the income for a period of time, there is really not a present gift being made. There is no "present interest." The beneficiary of the trust must wait until the period elapses to get the full rights under the trust. Your right to income comes first.

Because of this, the Internal Revenue Code considers a transfer to a GRIT, GRAT or GRUT only a partial gift. It calculates the percentage of the assets gifted for tax purposes according to the number of years you are entitled to get the income and the amount of asset you get each year.

The Internal Revenue Code bases the percentage that you are expected to derive from the trust on the monthly interest rates on federal securities. Only a professional can make the calculation for you. But, here are some examples:

A 10-year GRAT paying 6 percent interest to the grantor would cause only 64 percent of the assets to be counted in the grantor's estate in determining estate taxes.

A 10-year GRAT at 9 percent would result in 46 percent of its value being included. A 20-year, 9 percent GRUT would have only 15 percent included.

A 20-year, 12.25 percent GRAT would have no inclusion whatsoever. The amount transferred would be estate-tax-free, even though the grantor had the right to take income for a 20-year period.

Are we having fun yet?

What's the catch? You already know it. If you don't outlive the period, then all the assets are counted in your estate for tax calculation. That's why it's not recommended that an older or ill person set up a GRIT, GRAT or GRUT.

The trusts work well for those who would like three to 10 years of income and are in good health.

If you use a GRIT, GRAT or GRUT, you still get the $10,000 gift tax exclusion in addition to saving a percentage of the amount over the exclusion from estate tax.

## Things To Do

❑ Calculate your taxable estate.

❑ Determine whether heavy tax planning is required.

❑ Choose material and charitable beneficiaries where appropriate to reduce the adjusted gross estate.

❑ Transfer assets to an irrevocable trust to receive at least the $10,000 you are entitled to gift tax free each year.

❑ If you still need planning, consider a transfer of more than $10,000 to a trust.

❑ If you need income from the transferred funds, consider the GRAT or GRUT.

❑ If you have a primary residence you would like to transfer, use the GRIT.

# CHAPTER 7

# HOW A COUPLE CAN USE THE SUPERCLAUSE TO SAVE $192,800 IN TAXES

In the section on taxes, you already learned that there is an unlimited marital deduction on estate taxes. This means that a husband or wife can leave any amount of assets to each other estate-tax-free. Yes, even millions of dollars! A husband or wife can also gift over any amount of money to each other during their lifetimes gift-tax-free. So far, so good.

Since most married couples plan to leave everything to each other and then to their children, the unlimited marital deduction works beautifully when the first one dies. No estate tax is paid at all on the federal level. Do be sure to check your state laws, which may be different from federal law. Even so, the state estate tax is usually small. It's worthwhile to concentrate on saving federal taxes first.

Despite the good news, the unlimited marital deduction causes a problem for the surviving spouse with assets of $600,000 or more accumulated over the couple's joint lifetime. The $600,000 need not be accumulated by the time the first spouse dies. Even if the survivor, by frugally saving or intelligently investing money, builds wealth after the death of the spouse, the use of the unlimited marital deduction can cost a lot in taxes. Here's how:

At the death of the first spouse, not only the marital deduction is available to save taxes, but the $600,000 credit is also available. Since all is left to the spouse, there is no taxable estate against which to apply the credit. The result? The credit remains unused. It is wasted. In the first estate there is no economic impact of the wasted credit. The results are felt in the second estate.

When the remaining spouse dies, he or she can take advantage of his or her own exemption; but, if taxable assets exceed the $600,000, a tax is imposed on every excess dollar. You may recall that the minimum federal estate tax is 37 percent and can go as high as 55 percent. It would be nice if the exemption of the first to die could also be applied to save more tax.

There is a way of doing that—which requires the use of a special clause I call the *Superclause for couples*. In legalese it is called the *credit shelter clause*, the *unit trust clause*, and the *federal exemption clause*.

## Concept 31

### Understanding the Superclause

A Superclause provides that the surviving spouse will be the beneficiary of a trust. Instead of getting all the inheritance outright, $600,000 (or less, whichever is best suited to save the maximum in federal estate taxes) will be allocated to the trust created by the Superclause. The actual amount allocated is determined by the executor in consultation with the estate's accountant after the death of the first spouse. The Superclause is always written in general language; it never indicates a specific amount of money.

Under the trust created in the Superclause, the spouse is given the income from the trust for life; but, the principal goes to the couple's children at his or her death. Here's the punch line: Since the surviving spouse is not receiving the money outright, only in trust, the marital deduction does not apply. But, the $600,000 exemption does. In this way, while the tax in the first estate is the same with or without the Superclause, the tax in the second estate is greatly reduced.

This happens because the children, not the spouse, are deemed the inheritors of the money in the trust, even though Mom or Dad gets income. When the surviving spouse dies, the amount in the trust goes right to the children, the assets are not counted again in the survivor's estate, and no tax is paid. Here is an example:

- Gross estate of husband and wife is $1.2 million.
- Husband sets up a Superclause in his will or revocable trust.
- They divide the funds equally in separate names.
- After the husband's death the executor allocates $600,000 to the trust.
- The surviving wife still has her own $600,000 outright.
- No tax is paid at the husband's death, because the $600,000 is covered by the up-to-$600,000 exemption that everyone gets (this would have been wasted if there was no Superclause).
- The wife uses the income from all the money, but doesn't spend any principal.
- When Mom dies she leaves all of her $600,000 to the kids, tax-free, using her $600,000 exemption.
- The $600,000 in the trust goes to the kids, tax-free, under Dad's $600,000 exemption.

The result is that no tax was paid in either estate. Let's see how much the Superclause can really save.

---

### Concept 32

### The Superclause can save a family up to $192,800 in taxes

Once again, let's say dad left everything to Mom. If Mom, in turn, left everything to the children, there would be a tax when she died. Her estate would apply the $600,000 exemption, but there would still be $600,000 left on which to pay taxes. The tax on that amount is $192,800. If money held in treasury bills earned enough to double every 10 years, it would take the folks almost 50 years to accumulate that much money if they made an initial investment of $10,000.

So why doesn't everyone use a Superclause?

For the most part, wills are not reviewed frequently enough. The law changed in 1981. Before that, Superclauses were not popular. So many people who have failed to look at their estate plan over the past several years are not aware of what the clause can do.

Many people know about the clause and don't use it because they don't want to tie up any money in trust. They want the surviving spouse to be unhampered in receiving principal and not limited to income only. Many spouses would rather have free reign over both principal and income than save taxes for future generations. If you feel that way, too, there are two compromises you can make.

You can buy an economical joint and survivor life insurance policy to cover the $192,800 in extra taxes that would be paid without the Superclause (see Chapter 10, Concept 55). Or you can include a so-called *Crummey provision* in the trust. It allows the surviving spouse to withdraw from the trust up to 5 percent of the principal each year (see Chapter 9, Concept 49, for more on the Crummey provision).

## Concept 33
### Where to use the Superclause

A Superclause can be used in either a will or a trust. When used in a will, the clause usually precedes the residuary clause. Most attorneys are familiar with this. Some are less aware of the fact that clauses can also be included in revocable trusts. You do not have to give up a probate avoidance plan using revocable trusts because you would like to use a Superclause. The very same language used in a will can be incorporated in a revocable trust.

## Concept 34
### How to choose a trustee

Usually you will use family members as trustees for the trust created by the Superclause. Since such trustees are beneficiaries and usually serve without fee, this makes the trust even *more* super.

Your children can act as trustees even though they are the eventual beneficiaries of the principal of the trust.

Your spouse can serve as co-trustee even though he or she is the income beneficiary. However, the spouse must specifically be prohibited from electing to invade the trust for his or her own benefit. A non-spouse trustee can be given the power to use principal for the benefit of the spouse but he or she must have full discretion as to whether to use the funds. The spouse can have no say.

If you have a great deal of money or no proper trustee, a professional trustee can be named. See the criteria I recommend for your choice of a professional in Concept 9.

## Concept 35
### The QTIP Trust: misunderstood, misplaced and misogynistic

Too often confused with the Superclause is the QTIP Trust, which stands for Qualified Terminable Interest Property trust. These trusts do not save one dime in taxes. They do, however, allow you to tie the hands of your spouse and still have trust funds qualify for the unlimited marital deduction.

Yet, many lawyers, mostly male, automatically pair the Superclause trust with the QTIP, at least as far as the "little woman" is concerned.

The QTIP trust permits any amount of estate assets to be placed in trust for income to the surviving spouse. The beneficiary of the principal of the trust must be the heirs of the husband and wife. The essential rules follow:

- The surviving spouse has full use of income paid out at least annually.
- The trustee at its discretion can invade principal for the spouse.
- The property held in the trust must be income producing.

- The property is distributed to the named beneficiaries when the remaining spouse dies.
- The trust can provide that the tax attributed to it in the estate of the second spouse is paid out directly from the trust funds and not from any other estate assets.
- The trust can have the Crummey power.

As long as you follow these rules, the amount placed in the trust still qualifies for the unlimited marital deduction even though the spouse is only getting income for life and has no control over principal.

Often the first $600,000 in an estate is placed in the Superclause trust and the remainder in the QTIP. But, there is a big difference. The Superclause trust saves $192,800 in tax. The QTIP does not save anything, it just prevents taxation on assets placed in the trust. Giving the assets directly to the spouse would qualify for the same tax break. So why do it?

There are lots of legitimate reasons:

- The spouse may be incompetent or incapable of handling the assets.
- The spouse may be under the influence of one or more children to squander the assets.
- It may be a second marriage and the principal was acquired during the first marriage for the eventful benefit of the children of that marriage.
- There may be a divorce agreement that requires such a trust to protect children.

While all these are good reasons, there is another one that is not so good. Many attorneys and their male clients believe that woman just can't handle money. They set up a QTIP with the wife's knowledge and tell a little white lie. The lie is that the trust actually *saves* taxes. It doesn't. It just doesn't *incur* taxes.

The spouse, believing that there are taxes to be saved, consents to the QTIP arrangement rather than insisting on the outright receipt of the assets. She may not realize that her will has no such restriction on the husband; all of *her* money goes to *him* outright.

I don't mind the use of the QTIP. I do mind pulling the wool over the eyes of an uninformed party.

I hope the women reading this will be wise enough to pay attention to their estate plan and not to leave things solely up to their husbands, accountants, or attorneys.

## Concept 36
### The optimum use of the Superclause

Before we leave the topic of the Superclause, let's look at one more example of how it can save *hundreds of thousands* in federal estate taxes.

Let's say a couple has $1.2 million in joint assets. Everything is held in joint bank accounts, deeds and stock. When the first spouse dies, the survivor will inherit everything without probate (joint assets pass with no probate).

There will also be no estate tax because the unlimited marital deduction applies.

The problem arises in the second estate. Unless the survivor was a spendthrift, most of the principal is left. Applying the survivor's $600,000 exemption, there is a remaining $600,000 to be taxed. Total estate tax $192,800.

If, instead, the couple split up their holdings in separate names, each owning half the assets, then used a Superclause to create a credit shelter trust in their wills or revocable trusts, all that tax would be saved.

In that case, up to $600,000 would be placed in trust, income for life to the surviving spouse. That amount would be tax free. The remaining $600,000 would be left outright to the spouse in the residuary clause or in a QTIP trust. Either way the unlimited marital deduction applies.

When the surviving spouse dies, only the $600,000 not in the Superclause trust is taxable. The assets in the Superclause trust go directly to the children. They also avoid probate.

The overall tax saving is $192,800.

While this makes for good tax planning, please remember that even the most brilliantly drafted Superclause will not work if the husband and wife keep their assets in joint names. Joint accounts supercede both wills and trusts. So any assets in joint names will not be available to fund a super trust.

After you have completed your revocable will or trust, work with your attorney or paralegal to transfer assets into individual names so that the Superclause trust does not go unfunded.

---

## Things To Do

☐ Calculate your estate tax in the second estate.

☐ Recalculate using a Superclause that will preserve both exemptions.

☐ Discuss the wisdom of having a paid trustee vs. a family member.

☐ Examine your true feelings about not having total control of your assets.

☐ Check your wills and trusts for the Superclause. Have these amended if you wish to include one.

# CHAPTER 8

# SINGLE WITH CHILDREN: HOW SINGLE ESTATE PLANNERS CAN SAVE TAXES AND INCREASE PRESENT INCOME

In my seminars and during my radio shows, I am used to fielding questions from singles on saving estate taxes. For the most part, the questions ring of frustration and sometimes envy at the ease with which couples can strategize as compared to the divorced or widowed.

Many singles have children for whom they wish to provide. Others without close heirs are still loathe to give their hard-earned money to Uncle Sam. All singles are very concerned with increasing their own present income.

Fortunately, there is a special strategy that can work to meet two goals: estate tax savings and income tax savings. The strategy also increases the present income of the single planner. If it sounds too good to be true, let me tell you from the start that it involves the use of the unlimited charitable deduction, the purchase of an insurance policy, and a willingness to plan in an aggressive way.

## Concept 37
### The unlimited charitable deduction

Every taxpayer can give, during his or her lifetime or in a bequest at death, an unlimited amount of money to certain qualified charities and get a substantial tax benefit. If you are stumped over the tax definition of a charity or if you want to research the effectiveness of a charity and how much of your dollar will get where you want it to go, contact the National Charities Information Bureau, 19 Union Square West, New York, NY 10003-3395.

By now you may be thinking, I want to save taxes for my family. Charitable giving is nice, but charity begins at home. What's the strategy?

The strategy is to select a qualified charity. Then to set up a charitable trust under which you get the income from the assets that you transferred to the trust for your lifetime. The charity gets the money left in the trust at your death. Since there is an unlimited charitable deduction, all the money in the trust is estate-tax-free. As you can see, this gives you a way to reduce your estate taxes, even to zero.

Now here's how this benefits you by increasing your present income. If you transfer appreciated property to the trust as is, the charity can sell the property and invest it for you in certificates of deposit, bonds, treasuries or collateralized mortgage obligations.

You will receive more income than you would if you sold the asset yourself and reinvested it for income.

This is so because when you sell appreciated property yourself, you will first pay a capital gains tax upon the profit, whereas, the charity can sell the assets free of the tax. For example, if you bought 100 shares of AT&T at $25 a share and they are now worth $50 a share you would pay tax on $25 per share. This is the capital gain or profit you made. This tax can cost between 15 percent and 37 percent of the profit, depending on your federal income tax bracket and your state income tax bite.

If the charity sells these shares for you, *all* of the sale price, with *no* tax deduction equally can be reinvested for present income. If the gain was substantial, the difference in your monthly income will be substantial.

Further, when you create the trust, you will be getting a tax deduction. Any gift you give to a qualified charity is not only gift- and estate-tax-free, but, also a tax write off. This strategy, by itself, works very well if you have no heirs. You get a write off, more income, estate tax savings and help a worthwhile charity.

If you have heirs (here's the punch line), just replace the amount of assets you gave to the charitable trust with an insurance policy that gives them a death benefit equal to the amount you gave away. Obviously, the program has to be put together with a sharp pencil. This plan does nothing for you if you can't cover or nearly cover the cost of insurance with the extra income you receive.

## Concept 38

### Three types of charitable trusts that save estate and income taxes

There are many types of programs you can set up to get the double tax advantage of estate- and income-tax savings. Each can only be accomplished with the help of an attorney. The following concepts will prepare you for your consultation and familiarize you with the language used by lawyers and even charities when discussing estate planning.

Most religious institutions and large charities have planned-giving departments that can help you create your strategy. They often have in-house legal counsel that can draft the trust agreement and other necessary documents without cost to you.

If you have smaller charities in mind or want to name several different ones, you'll need your own separate counsel. If you are doing a tax, insurance and estate plan, I recommend you get your own attorney to work with the charity's lawyer.

Remember, these trusts are most useful from a tax point of view for singles with estate assets in excess of $600,000. There is usually a lot of tax savings hanging in the balance, so don't despair over the complexity. It's worth doing if you are a good candidate.

Here are some of the choices you'll encounter:

# Charitable lead trust

These trusts can be set up as irrevocable *inter vivos* trusts or as testamentary trusts in your will or in your probate-avoiding trust. The income from the trust goes to a named charity. The income is given to the charity only for a period of years. When the trust terminates, the principal goes to the beneficiaries, usually your loved ones—called the *remainder-men*. This is just like any other irrevocable trust, except that one of the beneficiaries is a charity.

Since the charity has the income for a period of years, the amount given to the ultimate remaindermen is diluted for awhile. Under the Internal Revenue Code, the result is a discount from the actual amount transferred. Less than 100 percent of the transferred assets will be used to calculate your estate tax. This saves taxes in the following way: Since the amount of the gift is reduced, the amount added to the gross estate as gifts given during your lifetime is also reduced. The smaller the gross estate plus gifts given, the smaller the ultimate tax will be.

## Charitable remainder unitrust

In this type of trust, the remainderman is the charity and your loved ones receive the income for a period of years, just the opposite of the lead trust. Often the income beneficiary is a loved one who cannot handle money because of a disability or an incapacity. The charity manages the trust, distributes income to the beneficiary for life, and gets the remainder when he or she dies.

This is useful for the single person who has no one in the family to help take care of the loved one after he or she is gone. It is also useful when the single person sets up the trust during his or her lifetime and has the charity manage the wealth for as long as he or she lives.

## Charitable remainder annuity trust

This version is the same as the unitrust except that the yearly distribution to the income beneficiary is never less than

5 percent of the fair market value of the asset when transferred into the trust. So the trust gives at least the same minimum amount to the income beneficiary each year.

These trusts save estate taxes because the majority of the gift goes to a charity and the charitable deduction from adjusted gross income applies.

## Concept 39
### How a single person can live on more because of charitable trusts

Charitable giving helps increase your income in two ways. First, when you give, you get a charitable deduction from your income tax.

Second, if you transfer assets that have increased in value to the trust, the trustee can sell the assets and will incur no capital gain. If you sold the asset at a profit you would have to pay the tax on the gain before you could reinvest the money for income.

For example, if you had 500 shares of AT&T that cost $10 a share and are now worth $50 per share, you would pay a tax on the $40 gain before you could buy bond, treasury note or other income-producing investments. The charity could sell the stock for $50 and pay no tax. The entire amount is reinvested for income production and paid out to you as income beneficiary.

## Concept 40
### Charitable giving and insurance

To make up for the amount you give to the charity, you can purchase an insurance policy equal to that amount and place it in an irrevocable trust. This keeps the proceeds out of your estate (see page 39), while giving you a charitable deduction.

For example, if a single mother has assets of $800,000 she will pay a tax on $200,000 (using her $600,000 exemption). This tax is approximately $74,000. If she buys a policy for $200,000 and leaves that in a trust for the kids irrevocably, they will inherit the amount estate-tax-free. If she also places $200,000 in a trust, keeping income for her lifetime and giving the remainder to the charity, she will get a useful charitable deduction from income tax. Further, if the $200,000 consisted of appreciated stock, a home or other appreciated assets she wanted to sell to reinvest for income, the charity trustee would sell it for her and avoid the capital gains tax on the profit. The extra income she gets from the deduction and investment of a greater amount of dollars may pay for the premiums and then some.

Your planner will work out the details to see if the program works for you.

---

## Things To Do

❑ Calculate your taxes under present conditions.
❑ Determine the cost of an insurance policy—ball park benefit amount is $100,000.
❑ Check out charities.

---

# PART 3

## LEGACY AND DYNASTY:
## HOW TO BUILD AN ESTATE AND KEEP
## IT FOR GENERATIONS TO COME

# CHAPTER 9

# DYNASTY PLANNING: BECAUSE A MIDDLE CLASS IS A TERRIBLE THING TO WASTE

So far you have received a basic education on how estate rules really work and how the wealthy stay that way. Chances are, if you're like me, you didn't start off with any money to protect. It's nice to know how to avoid *wasting* the money you accumulate for your family.

To add to your strategy, this Part gives you an estate planning program guaranteed (I mean that literally) to build a fortune for your family. By now, you are aware of my concern for the very existence of the American middle class. That means your family and mine. I believe that fortunes must not only be created for the moment, but for generations to come.

I have promised myself that I will never write a get-rich-quick book. This is about as close as I intend to come. It's a kind of get-rich-quick for the future. It will take you about two months to do all that is necessary to set the future generations of your family on the road to complete financial security. If, like most of us, you want your grandchildren to go to college and your children to have a comfortable life, you can provide it for them.

Hard work is not enough any more. To get ahead you need money from behind, and lots of it. This get-rich strategy is not for you directly (although I'll show you how to use the assets you accumulate in case an emergency arises).

## Concept 41
### Irrevocable insurance trust

You have already learned the concept of the irrevocable trust. An *irrevocable insurance trust*, as the name implies, is merely an irrevocable trust that holds an insurance policy as an asset. The policy may be the only asset, or it may be one among many. But, in any case, it is a special asset for estate and tax planning purposes.

## Concept 42
### Making an irrevocable insurance trust: A Dynasty trust

In a nutshell, to make an irrevocable life insurance trust into a Dynasty trust you and your attorney must imbue it with certain characteristics: 1) The death benefit from the policy must be kept entirely tax free of federal estate taxes. 2) The proceeds must go to your spouse, children, or whomever you choose. 3) If the policy has cash value, and you need to use it someday, you must be able to get your hands on the money. 4) If you want to build a Dynasty, you can have the death benefit managed and kept in trust for the benefit of grandchildren, and great-grandchildren, perhaps longer.

## Concept 43
### How do I get the money to buy a policy?

If you don't have the money to buy a policy but you own a home, consider a home equity loan to borrow the premiums. In this way, you can deduct the interest on the loan as an added benefit. Since home equity loans give you a line of credit, you can use the loan as needed each year to pay for the policy instead of taking a lump sum immediately. In this way, you will not pay any interest until you actually use the money.

If you don't own a home or don't want to borrow against it, you can use the term insurance from your job. If there is none, I will show you how to ask your employer to set up a special benefit at virtually no cost to him or her. Whatever the situation, this strategy will only work if there is a present or future insurance policy in the picture.

With the concept of irrevocable trusts firmly in mind and the willingness to use insurance for funding the trust, here are other concepts you'll need to implement the strategy.

## Concept 44

### Keeping the policy estate-tax-free for many generations

An insurance policy death benefit is an asset that is counted and taxed in your estate if you own it when you die. Ownership means that you are named as both the insured and owner of the policy even if your spouse, children or any other party are the beneficiaries. Chances are you expected your beneficiary to have use of the full death benefit. They won't if your estate is taxable and you die as the owner. In most cases, the death benefit from the policy will be taxed.

Even if you are not owner of the policy, but you control certain important elements regarding the policy, the death benefit is taxable. For example, if you still retain the right to change beneficiaries, determine how dividends are applied, borrow against the policy, or receive the cash value and surrender the policy, you are deemed in control. A controlled policy is an asset of yours and is counted in your estate no matter who is the official owner.

Most often, to be sure that your policy is out of your estate, you name the beneficiary (spouse, child, etc.) as owner. This is an irrevocable designation. When you die, the proceeds are distributed to the beneficiary tax free. But it does not create a Dynasty for generations to come. This is so because upon your beneficiary's death, the proceeds are taxed in his or her estate, unless, of course, the money is long gone.

To avoid taxation on the next death, use a trust as owner of the policy, with a trustee who can manage the proceeds for generations to come.

Eventually, the proceeds must be paid out in full. There is a rule against the dynastic accumulation of estate-tax-free assets—the *rule against perpetuities*. It requires that the trust terminate no later than 21 years after the death of the last possible person who could receive the funds under the terms of the trust. All attorneys either understand this requirement or have a software package that does.

The bottom line is that estate-tax-free wealth can be accumulated, in most cases, over three generations or more. While the amount you can accumulate through several generations, estate-tax-free is limited, the limit is so high that it will not affect the average middle class Dynasty builder.

## Concept 45

### Power of appointment: How to get a benefit out of the trust during your lifetime

Perhaps the biggest obstacle to creating an irrevocable life insurance trust, is that it is motivated by selflessness—a concern for building for the next generation and beyond. But what if you need the cash value that has accumulated? While some of you will be using group term insurance to fund the trust, most will use high-premium whole life, universal life, or the special joint and survivor life I will describe later. That's a lot of money going from your pocket into the future.

There is a clause that should be included in the Dynasty trust—*the power of appointment clause*—permitting you to enjoy the cash value of the policy during your lifetime under certain circumstances. This is the power to give someone else's property to another. If the property is in trust, it can be given back to the grantor or to a third party. Here is one version:

> During her life, the wife of the grantor shall have the power at any time and from time to time to make gifts of principal of this trust, in whole or in part, and in such proportions as she desires to the grantor or his issue, as she may set forth in writing.

The power is exercised entirely at the discretion of the holder of the power. The grantor has no right to insist on an invasion of principal. Finally, because the main asset of the Dynasty trust is an insurance policy, the only use you can make of it during your lifetime, or that a holder of a power of appointment can control, is to take out cash value or borrow against it.

Still, despite these restrictions, the clause serves a purpose in a time of need.

## Concept 46

### Beware: Keep the power of appointment "limited," not "general"

Leave proper drafting of the clause to your professional. But be aware that the power of appointment of the type I describe here is a "limited power of appointment." The asset over which the power may be exercised, and the people who may get the distribution, are specifically named in the document.

Check that the clause your attorney uses doesn't give a so-called "general power of appointment." This power, as the name implies, allows the holder to give funds to anyone and often covers a substantial portion of the grantor's assets.

This is both too broad for the control you plan to exercise and has a bad tax consequence for the power holder. The Internal Revenue Code deems a general power, but not a limited power, as a valuable asset of the holders. If the holder dies, the right to appoint is evaluated and included in his or her estate for estate tax purposes.

A power that allows assets to be given to the estate of the grantor or his or her creditors creates a general power. So be specific as to whom the holder of the power can distribute funds from the Dynasty trust. Be sure to coordinate the clause with the insurance policy you are using to fund the trust. Use the illustration that your insurance agent gives you to gauge the buildup of cash surrender value. If there is a lot of money at stake, be careful to pick a power holder in whom you have confidence. You need someone you trust to do the right thing if you need an invasion of principal.

## Concept 47

### The $10,000 gift package

The optimum amount of premium to spend yearly on a policy is $10,000 per beneficiary or $20,000 if you are a married couple. Don't faint. There are good tax reasons for this.

As you remember, each taxpayer may give a gift of $10,000 per beneficiary per year and that amount is entirely excluded from gift or estate tax. Married couples can give a joint gift of $20,000 per year.

While this is a lot of money, many people are fortunate enough to be able to make such gifts. But they are often concerned that the gift goes to buy more furniture, dinners out and vacations, not to fund and build future fortunes. The same gift transferred to a Dynasty trust to purchase a whopping insurance policy can create wealth *one hundred fold*.

Remember, if you already give a gift to a beneficiary, you are not entitled to give another excluded gift to the same beneficiary just because a trust receives the funds.

For example, let's say you have two sons, both of whom are beneficiaries of the Dynasty trust. One year the younger wishes to buy a house. To help him out you gift over $5,000. You cannot also give $10,000 to the trust and have it excluded from gift tax. You *can* give $5,000 to the trust for him and $10,000 to the trust for his older brother, both gift-tax free.

## Concept 48

### Giving amounts other than the excludable amount

If you plan to spend less in premiums than $10,000, 100 percent of your gift will qualify for the gift tax exclusion. If the premiums are more than the excluded amount, the gift will be taxed unless your total lifetime gifts and inheritance is under $600,000.

An interesting problem arises when you decide to transfer an existing policy with cash surrender value to a Dynasty trust. The Internal Revenue Code provides that the gift value is based on the policy's "interpolated internal value." What?

The "interpolated internal value" of a policy is a value too difficult for you or me to calculate. Luckily, our insurance agents can. It is partially based on the cash value built up in the policy. If that amount is under $10,000, the exclusion applies. If the amount is over $10,000 you may want to borrow against the cash value of the policy to reduce its value before you make the transfer.

## Concept 49

### The Crummey provision: Making sure your gift of premium is truly tax excludable

The Crummey provision is a masterful example of how understanding tax laws can bring a real benefit. As with so many tax matters, there is a roadblock in the Internal Revenue Code that could prevent a gift of premiums from qualifying as an excluded gift.

The Code only recognizes present gifts, gifts that can be used when transferred, as excludable. An insurance policy doesn't give the beneficiary anything until the future. If it or the premiums that pay for it are considered a future interest, they are not excludable from estate tax.

The Crummey case saves the day. It provides that a clause allowing the beneficiary to withdraw the *corpus* immediately creates a present interest in the gift, and therefore preserves excludability. The power to make a withdrawal can, by the terms of the trust, be limited to a short period of time each year. If the beneficiary passes up the chance to withdraw, the right is forfeited and the gift is excludable. This explains the odd language of the typical Crummey provision:

> Within a ten-day period of the receipt of any property placed in trust by the grantor, the trustee shall notify each beneficiary of the details of such receipt, whereupon the beneficiary shall have an unrestricted right to withdraw said funds for a period of six weeks, and the maximum amount receivable by any beneficiary under this provision shall be $5,000.

In practice, a few weeks before a premium is due, the grantor gifts the amount of the premium to the trust. Beneficiaries are notified. They pass up their right to withdraw. The trustee pays the premium when due. The beneficiaries can even be minors who lack understanding of their rights. Yet, under the legal rigmarole created under Crummey, the gift of premium is excludable if $10,000 or under. All's well that ends well.

## Concept 50

### New policies: Practical tax-wise procedure for setting up the trust and funding with insurance

If you are purchasing a policy solely to fund the Dynasty trust, make sure that the trust is in existence at the time of application. Don't buy the policy yourself, *then* transfer it to the trust. Why not?

Under the Internal Revenue Code, a policy transferred within three years of death is counted in the grantor's estate. Just the result you want to avoid. Should you buy the policy and die within the three-year period, the trust will be valid but the death benefit will be included in your gross estate.

So *before* you apply for a policy, have your trust agreement ready and, if possible, have the tax identification number ready, too. The insurance application will require it. If you don't have one yet, just write "pending."

In fact, it should be the trustee, not you, who signs the application. In his rush to make a sale, an insurance agent may urge you to buy the policy and transfer it later. Just beware of the three-year rule.

## Concept 51

### Existing policies: Practical tax-wise procedure for setting up the trust and funding with insurance

Another important consideration for those of you transferring whole life or universal life policies with cash surrender values is the potential for a gift tax. If the "interpolated internal value" of the policy is over $10,000, you will incur a tax. If the policy can be stripped of some of its value before the transfer by borrowing out cash value, do so.

Some grantors even add a slightly more remote beneficiary, like a niece or nephew, to the trust to add an extra $10,000 excludable gift. They may also arrange with their own sibling for him or her to give a mutual gift of the same amount to their own child. This is true intrafamily planning and works well with close families of some means.

Otherwise the procedure for the Dynasty trust remains the same, whether a new or existing policy is used: Be sure that the trust is in existence before the policy is transferred. Apply for a tax identification number. Contact your insurance agent and fill out the transfer documents. The trustee will also have to sign the application.

If the policy in existence is a term policy, once again, the same rules apply. Of course, the policy has no cash surrender value so you need not be concerned with gift tax liability. However, some tax specialists argue that since term is renewable every year, three years or five years, each renewal starts the three-year rule all over again. That would mean you must die during the last two years of a five year policy to ever be free of estate tax on the death benefit.

I disagree. To my thinking the initial transfer is all that counts and three years later you're safe. Nevertheless, include a trust provision that the trustee has sole control over the decision to renew. It is a further indication that you have relinquished control over the policy.

The real problem with term insurance and the Dynasty trust is that term usually is renewable only to age 70. But it can be a good way to start the trust in anticipation of buying whole life in the future.

If you presently have group term life insurance, it, too, can be the basis of a Dynasty trust. Your employee benefits administrator will give you transfer forms and require that you provide the company with a copy of the trust. I usually ask that the company agree to accept only the first and last pages, to maintain privacy.

## Concept 52
### Split dollar insurance

Obviously, the more funding you can contribute to the Dynasty trust, the more substantial a Dynasty you create.

A possible job benefit that your employer can contribute is the *split dollar insurance strategy*. If you are self-employed, you can do this through your own closed corporation.

Each year the employer provides a benefit equal to the cash value of the policy accumulated over the past year. The amount is used to pay the premium. If more is needed you pay the difference. If less is needed, then the employer contributes the premium amount. The employer's contribution is secured by the cash surrender value of the policy under an agreement.

When the employee dies, the amount contributed by the employer is returned to it. The remainder of the death benefit goes to the trust. In this way, the employer has given an interest-free, secured loan to the employee to pay for insurance. Sometimes a term policy is purchased to pay back just the amount of employer contribution so the trust receives the entire death benefit.

Warning: The premiums paid by the employer are taxable income to the employee. This is not true of simple group term insurance.

## Concept 53
### Private split dollar

Many of you have neither the clout nor inclination to negotiate split dollar with a reluctant employer. But there is a method to my madness in explaining it to you. Split dollar can be privately arranged outside the work place. Let's say you want your parents to set up a Dynasty trust for you or your children. Or, conversely, your parents want to help you create the trust with insurance on your life.

One way is to make outright gifts of the premiums. Another way is to set up a split dollar plan. In many cases, this is better because the premiums are secured and returnable to the contributor. This helps parents feel secure and also permits them to will their right to receive the money back to another sibling. Keeping legacies equal is often a concern of parents.

| **Concept 54** |

## Other purposes of the Dynasty trust

The Dynasty trust is an irrevocable life insurance trust with a focus on building for other generations. The traditional insurance trust is virtually identical, but was formed for other purposes that are merely extra added attractions to the Dynasty. Still, these purposes can be achieved in the Dynasty document.

### Pay taxes

The trustee can be given the power to lend death benefit proceeds to the grantor's estate to cover estate taxes due. This is particularly important where the assets are real estate or a family business and forced sales to pay taxes could be devastating.

### Avoid probate

The entire estate plan can be drafted in the Dynasty trust. Your will can state that all assets not in the Dynasty trust be placed in the trust and administered under its terms. This is called a *pour over* will. The trustee would follow the trust provisions regarding distribution. In this way, the Dynasty trust is not a separate document but the essential document in the estate plan.

### Special needs provisions

The trust could also make a special college or medical provision for grandchildren or special heirs.

## Incapacitated heir

The trustee could be empowered to use trust funds to buy a lifetime annuity for an incapacitated spouse or adult child.

In short, any purpose that can be served by an irrevocable trust can also be served by a Dynasty trust.

---

### **Things To Do**

❑ Talk openly about gift-giving.

❑ Find out what your children have done with past gifts given to them.

❑ Determine if you would like to provide for grand-children or children only.

❑ Check all assets ready for transfer.

---

# CHAPTER 10

# LEGACY PLANNING: A SPECIAL TOOL FOR COUPLES AND BUSINESS PARTNERS

Using insurance to pay taxes, fund a Dynasty trust, or create an estate is wonderful—except for the cost of insurance. That's why opportunities to buy a policy economically are so welcome. In the past several years, a new type of policy called a *second-to-die* or a *joint-and-survivor* policy, has been marketed to couples or business partners that significantly cuts down insurance costs.

The premiums for these policies are based on joint lives, because the death benefit isn't paid until *both* insureds have died. The policies are meant to be purchased by high-ticket consumers for upscale purposes, such as paying estate taxes for the couple with more than $1.2 million.

But they're also very attractive: 1) for couples who do not want a credit shelter trust and would like $192,000 of extra insurance to pay taxes in the second estate; and 2) business partners or married couples who have small estates and would like to channel dollars for future generations into a Dynasty trust.

There are some bottom-line reasons that this type of insurance, which I call *Legacy*, is more economical than most whole life policies:

- The death benefit is not paid until both joint insureds die; therefore the date of death assumptions used to determine the premiums are based on joint ages. This makes the premiums *less* for the same amount of death benefit.

- A younger partner can save considerable dollars on the combined premium.
- Medical underwriting is less severe because two lives are involved.
- The policy is composed of whole life and term in varying degrees depending upon how it is designed. (NOTE: the buildup of cash value is not as great because of the term feature.)
- The policy is more easily available to older insureds than a single life policy.

## Concept 55

### The most important questions to ask about second-to-die policies

Second-to-die insurance is economical but can still be expensive if you plan to build a sizable estate. To sell the policy, the agent will always illustrate a method whereby the number of years over which you pay the premium can be limited, usually 7-9 years. After that, the premiums are paid from the cash account in which dividends have been deposited through the years. You can "vanish" the premium in more or less time, depending on the yearly premium you can afford.

A premium that is larger will build up more dividends and allow for the vanish more quickly. A smaller yearly premium will require more years of payment. In the long run, the total dollars spent on the policy is less if you pay more up front for fewer years. But you may not be able to fit large premiums into your budget.

In either case, the number of years the premium takes to vanish is based on an assumption as to the amount of interest it will earn. This assumption should be based on the past performance of the company, but cannot be a guarantee of future performance. Further, some aggressive salespeople will use a rate in excess of the past performance of their company.

To get a better picture, ask for an illustration showing the vanish date if the projected interest rate drops by 1 percent, 2 percent, 3 percent. Remember, the agent just uses his or her computer; you are only asking them to do their job.

Explore what options are available if the rate drops after a vanish. Will there be a decreased death benefit, resumed premium payment, or a shorter coverage period? Will the trustee be able to select the option? (The trust should give this power.) Not only price but cash value depends on the mortality tables used by the company to judge their risk in issuing the policy. Most policies of this type provide an increase in the cash value after the death of the first insured.

Ask the agent to run illustrations based on parties living to 100 and another based on the oldest dying at actuarial life expectancy. Policies may differ as to the extent that the first death affects buildup of cash surrender values.

## Concept 56

### Is your insurance and annuity company safe?

In the aftermath of the savings and loan failures, most of us worry about the financial strength of other major institutions like insurance and annuity companies. Yet with interest rates way down and baby boomers trying to make up for lost time, our investment attention is turned to many of the products offered only through insurance companies. The second to die policies are so high ticket and long-term that safety is of the utmost importance.

Insurance companies are rated by several independent services—A.M. Best, Standard and Poor's, Moody's and Weiss. In the past, Best rated insurance companies according to the following code:

| | |
|---|---|
| A+ | Superior |
| A and A- | Excellent |
| B+ | Very Good |
| B and B- | Good |
| C+ | Fairly good |
| C and C- | Fair |

Each rating would have additional footnotes, such as **c**—contingent on the occurrence of an event like a new owner or investor, **e**—parent company, not the company itself, has been rated, **p**—pooled ratings with related companies, **r**—reinsured ratings (other companies pick up large policies and reinsure them for the company), **w**—watched (the company's ratings are being watched for change), **x**—revised ratings.

At one time, an A+ rating from Best was enough to make you feel comfortable. Unfortunately, recent newspapers have revealed that Best will no longer publish negative footnotes that come with its ratings. Therefore, if a rating may change shortly, you will not know. The rating will remain until an actual change. For this reason I can no longer advise that a Best rating is enough to judge safety.

For the most part, a company rated by Best receives a good rating or no rating at all. In 1989, 259 companies received an A+ rating. In the 10 years prior to that, only 103 companies received such a rating. Given this state of affairs, what we are now left with is reliance on several smaller rating services that we can use to cross check each other. Here are the pros and cons of some of them, by no means an exhaustive list:

**Townsend and Schupp**—Ranks 75 mutual life companies into 10 categories including where assets are invested, pre-tax earnings, debts, and dividend performance. They publish a company-ranking service called LIBRA.

**Moody's**—Ranks 46 to 50 companies from Aaa down to C.

**Duff and Phelps**—Ranks 28 to 35 companies, usually giving a top rating to half a dozen.

**Standard and Poor's**—Ranks 75 companies on their claims paying ability from AAA to D. Over half the companies are rated triple A.

Companies must pay to be rated by these services. While this does not impugn the ratings objectively, it does, sometimes, mean that the companies likely to get high ratings are the ones that are rated in the first place.

The National Association of Insurance Commissioners provides an Insurance Regulatory Information System. Its purpose is to help state departments of insurance regulate the industry. The system is based on certain standards of financial condition—the ratio of commissions to expenses, the ratio of real estate owned to other capital, surplus' adequacy of investment income, and more. Your state insurance department will tell you which companies are out of the normal range and in which categories.

No company will be perfect on everyone's score board. I have developed my own criteria:

**1. Surplus**—The excess of assets over liabilities. If the surplus is high, the likelihood of insolvency is low. Check the Mandatory Securities Reserve (MSVR), the amount set aside to compensate for losses. The ratio of surplus + MSVR to assets should be 6% or better. Note the history of the surplus.

**2. Types of assets**—High grade bonds should account for 50% of the portfolio, junk bonds a minimum, mortgages no more than 25% and only on real estate. Stocks, real estate and cash, under 10% each. One sixth of assets in separate accounts are separately managed. These may have high quality common stock used to fund annuities, variable life policies and pension plans. If you purchase any of these, the history of the separate account is of crucial importance.

**3. Income trend and investment return**—How the companies investments are faring this year and the past 5 years.

**4. Dividends paid vs. earnings**—High dividends can stem from good investment performance or taking money from surplus and depleting it. Check the dividends and from where they are paid.

**5. Loans against policies are listed as assets**—They can be good assets if they're made at high rates. Check the volume of low rate old loans.

**6. Claims** collected compared with premiums collected.

**7. Persistency**—How many cancel their policies per year?

The answers to all of these questions can be obtained by reading the rating service reports, all of which should be available from your insurance company, local library and/or rural extension services.

# PART 4

## REAL ESTATE

# CHAPTER 11

# REAL ESTATE: FROM FUNDING YOUR RETIREMENT TO SAVING ESTATE TAXES

Today more people fund their retirement through the equity in their home than in any other way. Especially those people who never did get that solid corporate pension behind them. They are retiring into a better lifestyle than they ever expected, because the value of their home or other real estate has appreciated so astronomically. The impact of a real estate investment can even linger into the next generation.

The questions and issues involved in building a real estate investment into a Dynasty are many.

## Concept 57
### Types of interests in real estate

The most traditional way of owning real estate is called *fee simple absolute*. This concept of ownership dates back to medieval times when landowning lords protected their complete control of their property:

It is the way we own real estate when our name alone is on the deed. We can mortgage, sell, tranfer, will, gift over or place the real estate in trust with no restrictions. The deed is registered in the county clerk's office, giving notice to all parties that we own the real estate.

Another way of owning property is the *lease hold*. You don't actually own the real estate—you have the right to the exclusive use and possession of the real estate while the lease lasts. Usually you have rights to sublet or sublease the real estate, giving you the right to the rent of that real estate. While income can be derived by owning a lease hold, the appreciation in the property is never your own.

A third way of owning real estate is to own a *life tenancy*. That means that you can stay in that real estate, use it for yourself, rent it to others, but only for your natural life. When you die the remainder of that real estate goes to another person or another entity.

*Remainder interest* is another type of real estate ownership. This means that you cannot rent or use the property for a period of time, perhaps for the lifetime of the life tenant. But you do get the real estate when their life tenancy terminates. That makes you the remainderman. Appreciation in the property as it accumulates becomes yours when you get it.

A *reversion* or a *reversionary interest* means that you had owned the real estate, gave it up or gave away a life tenancy to someone else. But under certain circumstances the whole parcel of property will revert back to you. For example, perhaps you sold the real estate, contingent upon its use only as a state park. If it is ever used for a different purpose, it will revert back to you or your family.

Finally, owning real estate as part of a *constructive trust* is something that usually a court has to pronounce. Here's an example: You helped someone fix up a piece of real estate and received no payment for it. Your understanding was that you would own half, but the other party never transferred any of the ownership on the deed to you. Or perhaps you joined a partnership and put in value in both cash and work and yet the title doesn't reflect your ownership. A court can name the owner of record as a trustee for you, holding that real estate for you in a constructive trust.

---

### Concept 58

### Joint ownership: Tenancy in common

Joint ownerships are types of fee simple absolute ownership where more than one party has an interest in the real estate. A *tenancy in common* is created when two or more people jointly own the property such that each of them is an owner of an equal share in the property. This means that they can leave their fractional share to their heirs or give their fractional shares away or pledge them for credit without the knowledge and consent of co-owners in common.

Sometimes this makes the owners very happy. Sometimes they own in common unwittingly, and a disaster occurs. For example, two sisters have lived in a home all of their lives, each contributing equally to the upkeep. The deed names both the two sisters individually. There was no explanation of how they owned. When a deed is silent it is presumed that they own as tenants in common.

What's the result? If one of them should die without a will, leaving nothing to the other, the half-share does not automatically go to the surviving sister. If there are other siblings, even children of other siblings, that half share, held in common, will be left according to state statute with the surviving sister taking only a small percentage of that half share along with other brothers and sisters and their kids.

Here is another example of a tenancy in common: Two friends who bought property would like to ensure that if anything should happen to one or the other, their respective families will inherit their half share. They also want the freedom to sell their half share if they find the proper buyer without the consent of the other. A tenancy in common is just right for them.

## Concept 59

### Joint ownership: Joint tenancy

Joint tenancy is another medieval concept in which both owners own the whole undivided interest. Neither can sell their property without the knowledge, consent and cooperation of the other. Should such a sale take place, the third party will not have marketable title without the agreement of the nonparticipating owner. Joint tenants cannot leave their property to anyone other than their joint owner, and if they do so the joint ownership supersedes the will. Often you will see on the face of the deed two names and then the form of words "As joint tenants" or "With right of surviorship" or "Jointly" or "As husband and wife" all of these form of words create a joint tenancy as opposed to a tenancy in common.

## Concept 60

### Condominiums: Common interest

In the modern days of condominiums, there is yet another way of owning property together called a common interest. I like to call it a *community* of interest because it is slightly different than a strict tenancy in common. With a condominium, the ownership may be fee simple, joint tenancy or tenancy in common. In addition to ownership over the condominium unit, there is ownership over the common elements in the building, such as elevators, swimming pool, lobby, perhaps the valet stand. How is this owned? By all of the owners in the entire building with a community of interest having a fractional share of these common elements and usually having to pay for their upkeep through monthly maintenance payments. When you buy a condominium you have both a real estate ownership in a unit and you are also a tenant in common with everyone else in the building.

As to the common elements in the building, co-ops are different. They are not real estate at all. Co-op owners actually own shares of stock in a corporation that owns the real estate. Transferring of shares may be restricted by co-op boards. But profit on the sale of co-ops are taxed in the same way as real estate.

## Concept 61

### How profits on real estate sales are taxed

When you sell real estate you will pay a capital gains tax on the profit. Here is how to calculate it: We begin first by taking the sales price: How much money did you get for your real estate? We deduct your purchase price, any improvements you may have put into the real estate through the years, and the closing costs in buying and in selling the property. The sum of these costs is called your basis, which is deducted from the sale price to determine your profit. Obviously, you want your sale price to be as high as possible. But, in order to save taxes, you also want your basis to be as high as possible. We would like the highest purchase price, the highest improvement and the highest closing costs.

Many people bought real estate in the 60s and the 70s and they paid very little for it compared to today. Their basis is low, their profit is high. Thus, their capital gains tax is high.

## Inherited property

There is a feature of the Internal Revenue Code that works only when property is received through inheritance rather than purchased or gifted. It is called the "stepped-up basis" and it allows for a "kinder" taxation on the inherited property.

Rather than using the purchase price as part of the basis, the IRS allows the property to be evaluated either at the time of the owner's death or six months later. The IRS permits either of those two evaluations. Whatever time is chosen, that market value is used for the basis.

A basis figured on current market value rather than using original purchase price will likely be much higher—and will result in a better tax advantage for the beneficiary.

When the person who inherits the property sells it, perhaps very soon after the death of the owner, the profit will be diminished for tax purposes because of the stepped-up basis. As you consider other ways to transfer property in your lifetime, remember that the advantages of stepped-up basis are only applicable if you are willing the property.

## Concept 62

### Gifting property: The fractional share

If you wish to break down the gifting of real estate to $10,000 units and take advantage of the gift tax exclusion, do it by the fractional share method.

You gift over a portion of the real estate by changing the deed every year and putting a fractional share on it for your kids or other donees. If you and your spouse own a commercial building, you might change that deed to give a tenth to your child and hold the other 90 percent by deed in your name. The problem with this is the ongoing necessity to transfer appropriate fractions, year after year, while making sure you stay within the bounds of the gift tax exclusion.

## Concept 63
### Gifting property: The corporate method

Another way to break down the value of real estate in tax excludable "bites" of $10,000 or $20,000 is to transfer real estate to a corporation, then give gifts of shares in the corporation. The shares of stock themselves can be transferred at the rate of $10,000 or $20,000 at a clip to your donee. In this way, without consistently changing the deeds and ownership of the property, you are transferring its ownership by stock transfers in a corporation that owns the real estate.

## Concept 64
### Transferring real estate: The partnership

A method of transferring property out of your estate and out of your income tax bracket is to establish a limited partnership and transfer the real estate to that partnership. You maintain an interest in it, and you give away the other interests to your donees. They become the limited partners and you become the general partner.

In this way real estate can also be transferred fractionally, as a part of the partnership is given up each year.

## Concept 65
### Transferring real estate through sales

You can sell your real estate to your donees and take back cash, notes or mortgages. Each year you can forgive a portion of those notes equaling $10,000 or $20,000 per couple. In this way, your beneficiaries own more each year without your having to change the title annually. Remember, forgiveness of notes for the sale of real estate to family members are under IRS scrutiny. There must be a true intent to have sold it in the first place, and the true intent to collect money from those people that you sell it to. However, just because there is a forgiveness of notes does not mean that intent is destroyed.

Check with your accountant and your attorney to prepare plans for implementing any of the Concepts 62 through 65. If you are successful in transferring the property from your estate, you will have saved estate taxes.

## Concept 66

### Balance the desire to save estate taxes against the loss of the stepped-up basis

If you already own property that has significantly appreciated, generally it should not be transferred. Instead, keep it in your estate and have your family enjoy the benefits of a stepped-up basis upon inheritance. But if your real estate has not yet appreciated, you might wish to shift it very quickly so that any of the appreciation that does accrue will not become part of your estate. If you transfer it to adult children in a lower tax bracket than yourself, all of the income from that property will be taxed at their lower bracket.

Often an estate tax on real estate results in the forced sale of the property. But if a corporation owns the property and your interest in the corporation is equal to or greater than 35 percent of your total estate, you get a tax break.

## Concept 67

### Trust ownership of real estate

When you transfer real estate to a trust, whether for management purposes, to avoid probate, or to see if you can shift the income to other family members, don't forget to check your mortgages to make sure that they will not be called if the transfer is made. And check your insurance policies to make sure that they will remain valid even if a transfer to a trust ownership is made. Is a trust a good vehicle for owning real estate? It is if your major goal is to avoid probate and a lesser goal is to make an irrevocable trust to take the property out of your estate. It is very important, even necessary, to establish a trust if you own property in states in which you do not reside. This is because probate, while it can be handled efficiently in your own state, can become expensive if it is multi-state. An ancillary proceeding, a special separate proceeding in every state in which you have real estate, will be required.

If, instead, you hold your out-of-state real estate in a trust valid in the state where the real estate is, whoever you designate as your trustee will be able to avoid the ancillary proceeding. They can transfer the real estate immediately to your other beneficiaries without going through probate. Of course, the trust could own the corporate stock or partnership interests as well.

## Concept 68

### The family real estate corporation

You already have purchased a viable piece of real estate. You see that it is going up in value. You are concerned that if something happens to you, Uncle Sam will take a big tax bite. You're also concerned that the income from the property is being taxed highly on your personal income tax return. Management is needed, work is needed, and your family (daughters, sons, others) are beginning to build the family fortune. What should you do?

Transfer the ownership of the real estate to a corporation that is created in the state where you reside. Two types of stocks are issued: common stock and preferred stock. The common stock is given to your children. You keep the preferred stock. You have all of the voting rights and you continue to manage and make all the decisions regarding the property. You also get all of the dividends from any distribution to stockholders. You also have a "right of redemption."

That means that your preferred shares can be turned back to the corporation and redeemed for cash. If cash accumulates in the corporation you can relinquish your shares of stock; perhaps when you are ready to retire and cash out.

There are formulas for doing this: You must use an attorney and an accountant. Meanwhile, common stock is owned by your family members. Because they own the common stock in the corporation and the corporation owns the real estate, any appreciation of the real estate is charged to the corporation. When you die, the value of the common stock will not be part of your estate. In addition, if you or your family members are employees of the corporation, you will be drawing a salary and some of the income derived from that real estate will be paid out to you as salary.

In sum, you purchase real estate, you get dividends from it. you draw a salary from the income it may be producing. If you die, it is not part of your estate for estate tax purposes.

## Concept 69

### Family real estate: The limited partnership

You as head of the family have purchased real estate. It will most likely appreciate; perhaps it has done so already. Instead of transferring it to family members, and then relinquishing all control, you can transfer it to a limited partnership. This freezes the value of its appreciation in the estate to one value as of one date of transfer. A partnership agreement is drawn at arms length between the limited and general partners. The general partner (most likely you) has the right to run the real estate and the real estate business.

You also have a right to take income from the partnership to make up any deficiency in a salary you draw for management. It is only this amount in the capital account of the partnership that becomes a part of the estate. All of the appreciation in that real estate is not added to your capital account. Instead it is added to the capital account of the limited partners who are family members. Once again, upon death, very little is added to the decedent's estate for tax purposes. The partnership continues after the establishment of a new general partner as provided for in the partnership agreement.

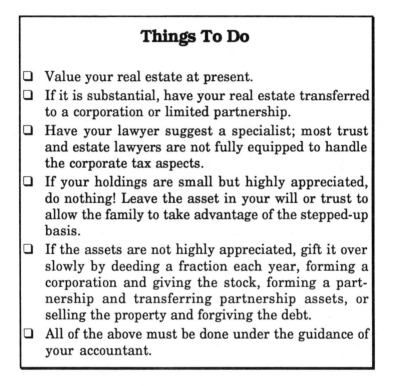

## Things To Do

☐ Value your real estate at present.

☐ If it is substantial, have your real estate transferred to a corporation or limited partnership.

☐ Have your lawyer suggest a specialist; most trust and estate lawyers are not fully equipped to handle the corporate tax aspects.

☐ If your holdings are small but highly appreciated, do nothing! Leave the asset in your will or trust to allow the family to take advantage of the stepped-up basis.

☐ If the assets are not highly appreciated, gift it over slowly by deeding a fraction each year, forming a corporation and giving the stock, forming a partnership and transferring partnership assets, or selling the property and forgiving the debt.

☐ All of the above must be done under the guidance of your accountant.

# PART 5

## A FAMILY AFFAIR: DON'T LOSE YOUR HARD-EARNED MONEY TO A FAMILY CRISIS

This book is about estate planning. And you have already learned how far-reaching the topic is. That's why it is appropriate to address certain special events and situations that may affect your family even though they have nothing directly to do with trusts, wills or probate.

Among such situations may be divorce and remarriage, debts and creditors, and mental illness. Of course we'll deal with each topic from an estate planning point of view. But you'll be surprised at just how helpful that point of view can be in coping with the *overall* situation.

# CHAPTER 12

# ESTATE PLANNING: DIVORCE AND REMARRIAGE

At least 20 percent of the questions I get during my radio and television appearances are related to protecting assets in the event of a divorce or a second marriage. In both cases, estate planning can help *prevent* damage, but cannot cure it. That means that planning is best done before and during the marriage. Since nothing has happened yet to warrant concern, attention to these matters can cause friction at home and have a chilling affect on the romance.

I have been a divorce lawyer and a divorce mediator for many years. I have trained and lectured numerous groups of psychologists and psychiatrists on the topic of divorce and money. And I have learned a few things from them and from my clients. Here are some tips on handling this intimate subject while the marriage is still "good:"

- Don't be a sneak. Tell your mate what you are doing and why.
- Give equal opportunity. Work with your mate to protect his or her assets as well.
- Be specific. Know what assets you want to protect, and handle them individually.
- Examine your suspicions. If you suspect that your spouse doesn't consider you an equal, or is hiding assets, deal with it openly.
- Don't imitate others. Times have changed and all couples are different, so don't listen to friends or family about how to deal with *your* situation.

- Remember, you have the right to protect yourself and your children—know the rules.

In the next several concepts, we will learn those rules and explore how you can help yourself and your family from an estate-planning point of view.

## Concept 70

### Family assets your spouse can get in the event of a divorce

The division of assets upon divorce or separation is a matter of state law. To properly protect gifts, inheritance and other assets, you must consult an attorney.

Recently, the Catholic Archdiocese of New York asked me to participate in a video about money to be presented to pre-marrieds. I was happy to get involved because I believe that, despite the "wet blanket" it may throw on the glamour of the wedding preparations, it's important for couples to get the full story about their legal rights.

Accept the following as a thumbnail sketch, applicable in most states, under most circumstances. But remember, it is just a broad overview—get specific advice for yourself from a divorce lawyer, even if the marriage is fine.

In most states when there is a divorce proceeding, the judge is empowered to distribute marital property "equitably." That is why the law is called "equitable distribution." The rules give judges a lot of leeway in judgement. He or she can consider the length of the marriage, the age and health of the parties, the contribution in money and services made by the parties to the marriage, lifestyle and custody arrangements.

The courts can also consider other wealth called "non-marital assets" in determining equitable distribution. Non-marital assets include property accumulated before the marriage, and gifts or inheritance received before or during the marriage.

Please note an important distinction here: While the court can consider these assets in dividing up other assets or in awarding support or maintenance, it cannot divide up these non-marital assets and actually give them to the non-owner spouse.

For example, Mary inherits $100,000 in the fifth year of the marriage. In the tenth year, she goes through a divorce. The money has grown in a separate account in her name and is then worth $175,000. The court will consider all the original inheritance and all of its growth as a non-marital asset. Her husband will receive none of it. But Mary is required to disclose the fact that she has this asset. The court can consider non-marital wealth in determining child support and maintenance (alimony). In some states, the court can consider such wealth in dividing up marital property, although it cannot distribute the non-marital property *per se*. As a practical matter, even in jurisdictions where non-marital assets are not relevant, they can influence a judge in making an award.

## Concept 71

### Giving and receiving gifts and inheritance

#### Giving

In giving a gift or making a bequest in a will or trust to an adult child who is married, be absolutely clear that the asset is for your heir, not for the couple. For example, if you help the couple with a down payment on their first home, make the check out to *only your child*, not to both of them.

In the event of a divorce, the gift and what was bought with it will belong to your child alone.

If a gift is very substantial, don't give it, lend it. Get a legally enforceable note from the couple, charge interest, and get collateral, if possible. For example, a parent can take a mortgage on a home or a lien on a car.

If you decide not to do this for emotional reasons, that's fine. But don't expect to get money back in the event of a divorce.

If you leave a bequest in a will or any trust to a minor child or grandchild, take care to include a trust clause. You must name a trustee, or an ex-spouse will end up in control of the assets if the custodial parent (you or your adult child) dies.

If you don't, the legal custodian will most likely be awarded the job by the court. Believe it or not, there have even been cases where husbands accused of killing their wives were given custody of children and became trustees of assets left to the kids by the deceased wife's parents!

### Receiving

Diligence must also be used in *receiving* a gift or inheritance. Keep the gift and all of its growth segregated. Assets that have been comingled with marital assets lose their separate "non-marital" character. When a divorce occurs, you may not be able to prove they are separate. Even if you have kept the assets in your name alone, that is not enough. Many types of marital assets that are subject to equitable distribution are also in only one name.

If your spouse handled, used, invested the money, or contributed to its growth, it can take on the appearance of a marital asset ripe for distribution.

If you want even greater protection, make an agreement in writing with your spouse-to-be to designate certain assets as non-marital.

## Concept 72

### What your spouse inherits when you die

In most states, you cannot disinherit a surviving spouse. If you do, he or she can elect to take his or her statutory share. This share varies slightly from state to state, but, for the most part it is one-third of your assets. In calculating those assets, everything you own, including joint assets with others, is counted.

Similarly, to count up the one-third, any assets left jointly to your spouse or in your will are counted. But not all trust assets are counted toward the one-third, even if your spouse is a beneficiary. He or she must get income from the trust at least yearly for it to be considered as part of the mandatory one-third.

In most states, if you give your spouse a sum of money outright (usually between $10,000 and $25,000, depending on the state) you can leave the remainder of the one-third in a trust. The trust can provide that the surviving spouse gets income for life and the principal goes to a different heir.

This is usually the most restricted way to leave the money.

The one-third is ironclad, even if the spouse was a louse. Wife beaters, adulterers and general nogoodniks all inherit. The divorce laws, not the estate laws, are to be used to take care of them.

If you want more restrictions you can use an antenuptial (prenuptial) agreement. These supersede the elective share rules of every state and are discussed in a concept to follow.

## Concept 73

### Remarriage and the marital home

Often in a second marriage the home in which the couple lives belongs to one of them. There may be a nuptial agreement relinquishing all inheritance rights to the home. Still, most owners will want to protect their spouses by providing them a place to live, in case *they* die before their spouses.

Homeowners *can* leave their homes to children of a first marriage or other heirs, and still ensure that their spouses continue to live in the house. The "life estate," which is created in a will, a living trust and on the deed, gives surviving spouses the right to stay in the home for their lifetimes. They can even rent the premises and use the proceeds to live elsewhere.

The surviving spouse cannot sell it or leave it to others. Upon the death of the spouse, the other heirs automatically inherit the home.

While the second spouse occupies the home, he or she is a fiduciary. The spouse must keep up the property and not allow it to deteriorate. The mortgage and other upkeep costs of the home can be paid for by the spouse, heirs or by a trust set up for that purpose. The will or trust should set up the plan for payment, or the spouse may be forced to leave and rent the premises to maintain its upkeep.

---

## Concept 74

### Antenuptial agreements

The law has a poetic and telling phrase for antenuptial agreements (also called prenuptial agreements). They are said to have a "chilling effect on the personal relationship of the parties." Still, with all the "chill" in the air over finances these days, and all the fears caused by alimony, galimony, and palimony, antenuptial agreements are having a heyday. Mind you, the word is **ante,** meaning "coming before or prior to," not **anti,** meaning "against or adverse to." Traditionally, couples have signed antenuptial agreements prior to marriage in order to define the financial arrangements they will have throughout the years. But antenuptial agreements can be signed during marriage, as well.

In America, antenuptial agreements were used mostly by wealthy families with daughters. There were two reasons, one social, the other historical. Historically, until the Married Women's Property Act of 1848, a women's property, upon marriage, was transferred to her husband. If she stayed unwed all her life, she was perfectly entitled to hold money, use it, run a business, manage investments and more. If she married, she surrendered her independence: The law no longer held her fit to handle the finances.

The scoundrel who married a woman for her money knew what he was doing. He didn't even have to wait until her death to inherit. When they married, her money became his and any business that she managed became his, too. If she was an heiress, the husband could take charge of her wealth the instant she claimed her inheritance. Naturally the wealthy worried that their children would be courted and married solely for their money. Fears of intrigue, possibilities of murder, or of commitment to a mental institution tortured their minds. They wanted to devise a way to protect their children from this manipulation. Thus, the antenuptial agreement.

Today, this agreement, signed by both parties and notarized, protects men *and* women. In most states it is acknowledged as if it were a deed. It need not be filed with the court. The contract relates exactly how the parties will hold property during the course of their marriage. It also frequently waives any rights of inheritance that a partner may have. To cap it off, there can be and frequently is a release of any spousal or marital share in the other's estate. This means when one spouse dies, the other won't inherit anything unless something's been provided for specifically in the will.

## Concept 75

### What can an antenuptial agreement do?

The antenuptial agreement can waive any rights that each spouse must, under state law, give to the other in their estate; yet it permits either spouse to *voluntarily* leave to the other as much as he or she wishes. If there is an ongoing business or other important income producer, the agreement can state who shall run the business or handle the investments and who shall receive the income or proceeds from it. The agreement can state that funds from a certain source belong to both parties equally or in different proportions. The parties can even agree on how they will spend certain sums throughout the course of the marriage.

Recently antenuptial agreements address financial issues pertaining to the event of divorce, as well as to death. This is a rather pessimistic approach to a new marriage; still, it can be very helpful, especially when one party has already been through a nasty and expensive divorce proceeding. There was a time (and it is still true in some states) when providing for the division of property and for support in the event of a divorce was against public policy. The theory was that this would encourage divorce and make it too easy. What has actually happened is that people are getting divorced more frequently despite the length and cost of divorce proceedings.

It may not be easy for a newly married couple to determine how they would like the finances to be distributed in the event of divorce or separation. But many people *do* know. Most important, it is not necessary that the contract cover everything. For example, if there is one major business or one particular trust fund or an upcoming inheritance or jewelry or other valuables being brought into the marriage, the contract can be addressed only to these assets. If there is a significant investment or business brought into the marriage by one party, the agreement can specifically state that the other has no right to control the particular asset or any profits derived from it.

Another possible clause is a waiver of support—or alimony. With the numbers of working women increasing, the issue of alimony and maintenance for women seems to be diminishing. Many couples agree to waive their rights of support (a man has a right from a woman these days) in the antenuptial agreement. This means that both parties will have an incentive throughout the marriage to accumulate their own wealth and to follow their own careers since they have waived their right to spousal support in the event of a divorce. Such waivers must be fair, or they can be set aside.

If circumstances change and a spouse becomes disabled, unemployed or in danger of becoming a public charge, the agreement can sometimes be set aside. Such a case is very difficult to prove and must show that such a circumstance could not have been foreseen when the agreement was signed.

## Concept 76

### To make the agreements ironclad, get a lawyer and disclose the facts

Antenuptial agreements certainly require counsel. In fact, one of many ways of setting them aside is to claim that one of the signing parties did not understand the terms and did not realize what he or she was doing. If there is counsel on only one side, it is very easy to show that the party without a lawyer was not represented. The party may have understood it perfectly but, in later years, may want out and claim ignorance. In some cases, the claim is perfectly true. One client of mine was himself a lawyer, but he worked in the Judge Advocate's office in the United States Army and knew as little about this aspect of law as any layperson. The wife had been represented by a high-powered attorney, and the husband had signed an agreement allotting an exorbitant amount of money to the wife in the event of divorce. Instead of waiving rights, she was *demanding* rights in the agreement.

Another requirement, other than being well-represented, is that there be a full disclosure of assets and income. The law wants to prevent people from giving up rights to money they don't even know exists.

---

## Things To Do

❑  List assets you would like to protect.

❑  Discuss antenuptial agreements or amend your will to give a restricted elective share.

❑  Make sure that all non-marital assets are segregated.

❑  Think before you give a gift to a couple in both their names.

---

# CHAPTER 13

# PROVIDING FOR AN INCOMPETENT ADULT CHILD

One of the most difficult areas of estate planning is providing for the adult child who has always been unable to handle finances because of a mental handicap or illness. Many parents also want to protect their assets from the adult child who is a drug addict, alcoholic or poor money-manager.

There are three possible solutions:

- disinheritance
- sprinkling trusts
- lifetime annuities

Because such an adult child may well squander or lose the money immediately, an outright gift is out of the question.

There is no need to devote further discussion to disinheritance. The proper clause to use in a will or trust is called the *in terrorem* clause and was discussed earlier in this book.

Sprinkling trusts and lifetime annuities, however, are lesser-known alternatives that can be real problem solvers.

## Concept 77
### Sprinkling trusts

A sprinkling trust can be set up in your will or living trust to take effect upon your death. It can also be set up as a living irrevocable trust if you want to transfer assets permanently during your lifetime.

The only difference between this type of trust and any other is that the trustee is given special powers to "sprinkle" the income among a number of beneficiaries named in the trust. For example, a competent and an incompetent sibling are named as beneficiaries. The trustee can distribute income yearly to one or both, in different proportions each year.

The rationale is to permit the trustee discretion to give or withhold funds, depending on the condition of the incompetent sibling. If the incompetent would be denied government aid if he or she received income or assets, then the trustee withholds funds. The remaining beneficiary is there to receive the funds.

This type of trust works well if there is a highly competent trustee. In this type of trust, I do not ordinarily recommend naming a sibling, friend or relative as a trustee. The caretaking aspect of the position is very wearing. The incompetent beneficiary can be demanding. The position of a sibling as a trustee and a beneficiary can cause conflicts that can last a lifetime. Often the family is best off with a bank or professional.

However, some planners do not have an independent trustee to name or do not have a large enough trust to warrant a professional and the fees they charge.

To them, I recommend getting in touch with charitable organizations related to the incompetent's problem. They can act as fiduciaries if they are also named as charitable beneficiaries.

## Concept 78
### Annuities for those who have no trustee

As a fallback position, it is worthwhile to explore a commercial annuity bought from an insurance company. An executor of a will or trustee of a revocable trust can be empowered to purchase an annuity that will pay the incompetent adult a lifetime income. The amount can be designated in the document.

An insurance professional can calculate for the fiduciary the amount that a lifetime annuity contract yielding the desired income would cost. The cost is based on the age of the annuitant (the incompetent adult) when the annuity is purchased.

The beneficiary will then receive regular income for life, and the parent needn't worry that the child will squander his inheritance.

On the negative side, the investment is unmonitored. If the insurance company should fail, or if paper work is necessary because of a change in organization, the adult incompetent will need help.

The most practical solution is to diversify among several companies. This is always a good idea when purchasing an annuity or large life insurance policy.

---

## Things To Do

❑ Consider creating a sprinkling trust if you have a trustee.

❑ If you have no trustee, do research on annuities.

❑ Be sure your will permits the executor to purchase annuities and, if so, share your research with your executor and successor executor. Don't name a specific company in the will or trust. Let the executor make the ultimate decision.

---

# CHAPTER 14

# DEBTS IN THE FAMILY

A "growth industry" in the 1990s appears to be the field of bankruptcy and asset protection. While this is a specialty beyond the scope of this book, there are some trust and estate concepts that will help save dollars and get you organized.

## Concept 79
### The debt clause in wills and trusts

All wills, and trusts that are designed to substitute for wills, have a clause that permits the fiduciary to pay the deceased's debts. Usually the clause merely provides for the paying of "just debts." Who is to say what is and is *not* "just?" I prefer to use the phrase "provable debts." This gives a legal definition to the term and also empowers the fiduciary to refuse payment if the debt is not legally provable.

A friend or relative who lent money, paid doctor bills or funeral expenses for the deceased, has the right to enter a claim against the estate. A fiduciary can refuse payment if the debt cannot be proved. An even stronger anti-creditor clause provides that only "legally enforceable debts" can be paid. In that case, any gift or gesture is not reimbursable.

## Concept 80
### The spendthrift clause

Often it is not the deceased who is a debtor; but, a beneficiary who is a *potential* debtor. To protect assets from a spendthrift, use a trust and include a special clause that prevents the beneficiary from using the future income or principal from the trust as collateral for a loan or purchase.

A creditor who accepts a future interest from a beneficiary with a spendthrift clause cannot collect if the beneficiary does not pay. The trustee can refuse to pay the creditor even if the debt is provable. The responsibility is on the creditor at the time of making the loan or transferring the goods to examine the beneficiary's interest in the trust.

## Concept 81

### The family limited partnership

Often people in vulnerable professions form a limited partnership naming their families as limited partners and themselves as general partners. Only the limited partners *own* the assets of the partnership; the general partners control the partnership and the investment.

For example, a doctor who may have major malpractice liability can form a family limited partnership naming himself as general partner and his wife and childen as limited partners. If a patient gets a judgement against him or her, they cannot collect from the assets contained in the partnership. They can place a charging lien on the doctor's share but can only take the assets when and if disbursed to the doctor himself, not the limited partners. If no assets are ever disbursed, they cannot be reached by the creditor. *Caveat*: This strategy may be set aside by a court if the general partner has already accumulated debt.

---

# Things To Do

- ❏ Check the debt payment clause in your will or trust. Change the language to "provable or enforceable debts."

- ❏ Investigate putting a spendthrift clause in your trust if you suspect one of your beneficiaries may have difficulty with debts.

- ❏ Consider creating a family limited partnership if you're in a profession with a high rate of lawsuits.

---

# PART 6

## ILLNESS, INCOMPETENCY, AND LONG-TERM HEALTH CARE

# CHAPTER 15

# NURSING HOME PAYMENT

"How can I protect myself from the catastrophic costs of catastrophic illness?" There isn't a more emotional subject nothing that concerns people more when addressing the protection of their assets. There's a lot to know, and I certainly don't propose to cover it all in this book. But I will answer some of the most frequently asked questions regarding powers of attorney, Medicaid coverage and eligibility, and mental competency.

## Concept 82

### Are there any assets that are protected in the event that I go into a nursing home?

A nursing home is like any other private institution. *You* are expected to pay. Some costs are handled by Medicare, which everyone is entitled to after age 65. Other costs may be handled by private insurance, presuming you've already bought some. If neither provides coverage, then you have to spend your own assets. Unless you seek Medicaid eligibility, the nature and extent of your assets remain irrelevant.

Medicaid is a poverty- or means-tested program. It is similar to welfare—the middle-class American is not eligible for Medicaid.

To determine your financial eligibility for Medicaid, a "snapshot" is taken on the day that you enter the nursing home or hospital, not the day that you applied for Medicaid, to identify your assets and to determine your eligibility.

Many of your assets may not exclude you from Medicaid eligibility. These "non-countable" assets might include: your home (if it's your primary residence), a cash amount (usually $2,000), a car (even an expensive one), personal jewelry, household effects (including art), prepaid funeral expenses, a burial account of up to $2,500, and term life insurance that has no cash surrender value. These non-countables are excluded from the snapshot.

Other assets *not* counted against you are called inaccessible assets—assets that would normally be considered, but because you can't get access to them, neither can Medicaid. What are they? Assets you've already given away, assets that you're holding in special trusts, certain types of joint accounts, and involuntary situations where you have become incompetent and you just cannot get a hold of your assets.

Your *countable* assets are what *keep* you from receiving Medicaid. These include cash over $2,000 (in most states), bonds, IRAs, Keoghs, CDs, treasury notes, savings bonds, vacation homes, whole life insurance policies that have cash surrender value, and every other asset that is not specifically listed as inaccessible or non-countable. In other words, just about all the types of assets you may have accumulated.

Sit down now with a pencil and paper and list what you have that is countable, non-countable and inaccessible. I would bet that most of your assets are of the countable variety, particularly your bonds, your CDs, and your CMOs.

## Concept 83

### Should I give my assets away and, if so, should it be in trust?

Before we answer that question, let's examine something called the *30-Month Rule*. If you're going into a nursing home and you transfer your countable assets to a child or other person prior to entering, you still have to pay the nursing home bills for a period ending 30 months after the transfer. For example, you transfer in September and go into the home in November. You must pay for 28 months. If the assets you transferred and your other countable assets run out before the 28 months are over, you become eligible for Medicaid.

Uncle Sam presumes that any transfer made 30 months or less before entering a home was made solely to qualify for Medicaid. This presumption can be overcome if you can show that you sold the property for its fair market value and the proceeds are still part of your countable assets, or if you had a legal obligation to make the transfer, for example, under a divorce decree or other contractual obligation.

You will also pay for less than 30 months under another portion of the 30-month rule, which says that if the average monthly nursing home cost in your area is determined by the Department of Public Welfare when divided into the amount you transferred is less than 30, you need only pay for that lesser number of months. Let me give you an example:

You have $100,000 in stocks and bonds, which you liquidate. You give $50,000 to your son and keep $50,000 yourself. You enter a nursing home in an area the Department of Public Welfare says averages $10,000 a month in nursing home costs. You divide the $50,000 you transferred to your son by $10,000. This indicates you have five months of nursing home costs you must pay before you become eligible for Medicaid.

Where do you pay it from? From the $50,000 that you've kept out of that $100,000 you originally liquidated. Once you've spent that $50,000, of course it's no longer a countable asset and you have basically impoverished yourself. Yet your son has kept $50,000 of your original $100,000. This can work well for you, depending on the numbers given to you by the Department of Public Welfare. It works especially well if you have no spouse, because a spouse gives you other kinds of protection.

## Concept 84

### Isn't there a type of trust I could use that shelters my money from Medicaid?

Maybe! There was a time when you could transfer assets into an irrevocable trust as long as the money was out of your control. There was a time that such a trust could give you back income, and even give the trustee power to invade the trust to pay for your health and welfare. Then if you needed a nursing home, the trustee would simply cut off any money he or she was giving you and you would be impoverished and eligible for Medicaid.

No more! If a trustee has any right to invade the trust for your purposes, the trust fund is considered countable and available to you even if the trustee doesn't do it—even if the trustee *refuses* to do it.

If you would like to transfer your funds to a trust in order to shelter them from Medicaid—and there are other good reasons to do that—be sure that the trustee has no power to distribute any of the assets to you for any reason. These trusts are simply irrevocable trusts with no power of invasion of principal for the benefit of the settlor.

Now what about income from the trust? You can permit the trustee to distribute income to you, but it still must be paid to the nursing home first. Medicaid will only make up the difference.

## Concept 85

### What if I simply transfer everything to my spouse, and he or she is well?

In 1988 the government passed the Spousal Impoverishment Act (SIA). I guess if they were more kind-hearted, they would have passed the "Spousal *Anti*-impoverishment Act." But they said exactly what they meant. Whether your assets are in you name, your spouse's name, or joint names, the Medicaid snapshot is a combined picture. It's taken on the day that the ill spouse either goes into a nursing home or into a hospital for at least a 30-day stay. The stay-at-home spouse may keep half of the total amount of the assets no matter whose name they're in, but not less than $13,296 and not more than $66,480. These figures go up a little bit every year and vary from state to state. These are ballpark figures, so research the specific rules in your state.

Does this mean that if you, as a couple, have assets of $200,000, the spouse who stays in the community can only keep about $66,000? That's right. The rest must be spent before there is Medicaid eligibility. Of course, if the ill spouse dies before the expenditure of that money, it will be inherited by or kept by the surviving spouse or children, depending on what trusts and wills provide.

Is there anything that a spouse can do? Yes, there is such a thing as spousal *refusal*. The spouse simply refuses to pay for nursing home expenses from assets that are in his or her name. What happens if a spouse refuses? Medicaid is allowed to bring a lawsuit. It is almost like a divorce proceeding for support. In fact, in many states, it is even held in the divorce courts or the support courts. Medicaid says that the spouse should be contributing more. The spouse says, "If there was a divorce or I needed support, I would be able to keep the amount of money that I'm planning to keep."

How do the courts rule? Most judges are middle-class people, earning an average of about $42,000 a year. They, too, plan to live a long time and maybe go into a nursing home. They did not make these laws. Most people report that they get a better break when they go to court for spousal refusal. It's up to you.

---

## Concept 86

### What about protection of income?

Some couples have very few assets but because of pension programs, Social Security or even jobs, they may have a great deal of income even after they reach 65. The Medicaid snapshot only includes the income of the person going into the nursing home. The income of the healthy spouse is not counted at all.

Therefore, if you can choose who is income beneficiary of a trust, annuity, or a particular asset, direct it to the spouse least likely to go into a nursing home. If you're both healthy, this may mean tossing a coin, but at least the odds are fifty-fifty that you'll guess right!

The spouse going into the nursing home has nearly every bit of his or her income counted: Social Security, rental units, pensions, annuities, help from family members, trusts, anything you could think of that's coming in on a monthly or periodic basis to them directly or with their name on it.

In most states, except for a small amount they're allowed to keep monthly, they must use the income to pay the nursing home bill. Only if the nursing home monthly bill exceeds the income will Medicaid chip in. Can they keep any? There are personal needs and home maintenance allowances, and a monthly premium to be paid for medical insurance.

The law requires that for joint income, the stay-at-home spouse is entitled to keep an allowance of between $856 and $1,662 per month. These figures vary between states. If it's income that you want to protect, here's how to do it: Be sure that as much of your income as possible is not in the name of the spouse going into the nursing home, reduce joint income and make sure you claim all the spousal allowances under your state's statute.

## Concept 87

### What happens to your home?

If you are a married couple, the person going into the nursing home can transfer it entirely to the name of the other spouse who in turn can transfer it to a child or another relative. Now the house is out of the name and ownership of *both* husband and wife and is fully protected.

Whether you are single or married, you can make a transfer of a house to: 1) a child who is blind, disabled or under the age of 21; 2) a sibling who owns a share of the home and has resided there for at least one year before the co-holder goes into a nursing home; 3) a child of any age who has resided in the home for at least two years before the parents go into a nursing home and can show he cared for them at home; 4) anyone, as long as you are selling it or transferring it for a fair market value and; 5) anyone else provided the purpose is not to qualify for Medicaid and the transfer is already part of an established estate plan. If no transfer has been made and a person dies owning a home, Medicaid can place a lien on that home. Consult an elder law attorney for more information.

# CHAPTER 16

# POWER OF ATTORNEY

The power of attorney, as with so many aspects of estate planning, was a tool for the wealthy to free them of the boring task of managing their wealth. Their attorney-in-fact, the legal name for a person holding a power, could attend a real estate closing for them in Paris, buy art at an auction, or negotiate the price of a yacht, all while they were on safari in Africa.

Today, this rich man's tool is a primary means of protecting your assets if you should become incompetent or incapacitated. The power of attorney is a document giving another individual legal authority to make financial decisions for you. This document can be a creative and useful tool for almost anyone. Let's see just what it can do.

## Concept 88

### There are several types of powers meeting different needs.

The most common power is the *limited* power of attorney. Like the rich man's power, it permits another person to act on your behalf, during your lifetime, in a limited capacity. For example, a limited power can permit someone to sign a specific contract for you, take out a loan with you as debtor, buy property, or sell stocks.

Many brokers and bankers are wary of these powers and would prefer to have the person who is the principal in the deal sign off personally. However, many times it is necessary to have such a limited power. For example, my client was about to attend the closing of her new house when she went into labor. The couple had already signed a power of attorney to permit the husband to close on behalf of himself and his wife. The birth and the real estate sale went off smoothly.

Another type of power is the *general* power of attorney. A general power of attorney permits the attorney-in-fact to do any act that the signer of the power could do. It is not limited to one category of activity. The usual 50-cent form you buy at a stationery store is a general power. It can be dangerous because, as long as you are alive and the power is not rescinded, the holder of the power can do virtually *anything* he or she wants with your money or property.

Both the limited and the general powers of attorney have these features in common:

- They are effective only during your lifetime.
- They are effective only as long as you are legally competent to act for yourself.
- They become ineffective if you become incompetent.
- They are effective as soon as signed.
- They can be revoked.
- You can name an attorney-in-fact and a successor in case the original person can no longer serve.

## Concept 89

### Powers of attorney can help if you become incompetent

As you can see, neither of these documents help you in the event you become incapable of handling your own money matters. The issue of incompetency planning has become a major concern as we live longer and accumulate more assets. The studies of aging show that it is a process during which we are in a dynamic state—sometimes capable of taking care of ourselves, sometimes not.

Anyone who has ever been a caretaker knows that older people can have better and worse days. Illnesses go in and out of remission. The ideal situation is for everyone to handle their own affairs, and to have a loved one take over only when this is out of the question.

The power of attorney can fulfill some of these needs. It can also take the place of an aggravating and expensive legal proceeding called a conservatorship proceeding.

## Concept 90

### Conservatorships

If a person becomes unable to handle his or her legal and financial affairs, a relative or other party in interest (including a governmental agency) can apply to the court to be named conservator. The word is a euphemism. Often very little is conserved and much is wasted.

Time is the first thing wasted. The person applying to the court must present his or her plan for the incompetent's welfare. Then the court must appoint a guardian *ad litem* (a stranger selected by the court from a group of approved attorneys) to guard the incompetent's rights. All the while, the wheels of justice slowly turn until the appointment is made— or the application is rejected. If this happens, the process starts all over again.

Money is the second thing wasted. There are court filing fees, attorneys' fees, and a separate fee to the guardian *ad litem*. The final thing wasted is emotions. The individual must be proved to be incompetent, and, in order to do so, is often questioned on the stand. The person applying for conservatorship is also under scrutiny to be sure his or her motives are honest. We wouldn't want the law any other way. But while you are competent and capable, it is better to choose your own representative and avoid the conservatorship process if the time ever comes that you cannot handle matters for yourself. Here's when the power of attorney comes in. Lately, special clauses have been added to make this document a better alternative than conservatorship proceedings.

## Concept 91

### The durable power of attorney

To make the power useful in case of incompetency, it must contain a clause stating that it remains effective in the event the maker of the power becomes incompetent. This type of power is called a durable power of attorney. It is not voided by incompetency or incapacity, whether mental or physical.

Careful selection of the attorney-in-fact is the essence of good planning. Each state has its own requirements. Most permit a family member, bank or professional to act. All permit the naming of a successor in the event the attorney-in-fact cannot serve. You may want to name two or more people to serve simultaneously, to provide checks and balances on each other. A durable power can give the attorney-in-fact the power to maintain the whole family in the manner to which they are accustomed, to spend money on everything from the family's teeth to car maintenance.

Since the powers are so broad, people want to be careful in determining *exactly* how the term incompetent is defined.

## Concept 92

### Springing power-of-attorney

A durable power of attorney is good as soon as it is signed. No incompetency or incapacity need be shown. The durability clause exists just to be sure that the incapacity doesn't void the power. It does not protect you from the attorney-in-fact using the power even if you are capable.

On the other hand, the *springing* power of attorney "springs to life" and becomes effective only when the tests for incompetency or incapacity are met. Further, a person, including the one who gave the power, can bring a court challenge against the use of the springing power, arguing that there is no incapacity. In this way, an attorney-in-fact who is acting wrongfully can be stopped from using the power unless he or she can prove that the signer truly is incompetent.

## Concept 93

### Working with banks and brokers

Many banks and brokerage firms use their own power of attorney forms and reject or discourage the use of your forms.

Check with your financial institutions at the time you execute a power, make separate ones for each using their forms. If you decide to name one child as attorney-in-fact for your bank accounts and another for your insurance policies or other assets, be sure you haven't granted them confusing or overlapping powers.

It is also very important that you ask the financial institutions whether they require a power of attorney to contain an indemnity clause relieving them of liability or expense arising out of the use of the power. If they do, either accommodate them or choose a different institution. Don't leave it to the attorney-in-fact to fight it out later.

## Concept 94
### Using powers of attorney with trusts

If you plan to name your spouse as attorney-in-fact and you have created a trust under which he or she is the beneficiary, make sure that your spouse isn't deemed to have the power to award themselves trust principal. This could spoil the tax plan, and, in some states, can even be prohibited. For example, if you are the trustee of a trust designed to pay your spouse income or principal, and you give your spouse a general power of attorney, he or she can act as trustee in your place. In many states, distributing principal or income to yourself is prohibited.

The solution is to create a limited power of attorney giving someone else the power to distribute trust funds to you or your spouse. Also, place a clause in the power that names your spouse stating that he or she cannot act on your behalf as trustee of a trust unless it so states in that document.

## Concept 95
### Revocable trusts and power of attorney

If you have made a revocable trust to avoid probate, you can couple it with a power of attorney to avoid separate documents and perhaps an additional attorney fee. Here's why: To be effective, the revocable trust must contain *all* of your assets. Anything not included in the trust does not avoid probate.

By creating a power, your attorney-in-fact can transfer anything you forgot to place in the trust, in the event you become incompetent and can't finalize the transfer yourself.

You can even leave the trust entirely unfunded. Place nothing in the trust (an *unfunded trust*.) If you become incompetent, the attorney-in-fact can transfer the assets and all the terms of the trust apply. The attorney-in-fact can also be named as trustee, or another person(s) or institution(s) can act as trustee.

Here is an example: A healthy 65-year-old trusts his spouse to leave matters in his hands unless he is truly incapacitated. However, if this happens, he wants his son and accountant to manage the money for the benefit of his wife and himself. He has his lawyer draw up two documents, a revocable trust and a limited springing power of attorney. He makes his wife the attorney-in-fact with the limited power to fund the revocable trust if he becomes unable to handle his affairs. He names the accountant and son as joint trustees of the revocable trust, but he puts no assets in the trust. All assets remain in his name and control until and unless he becomes incapacitated.

If he does, his wife transfers the assets to the trust and her role as attorney-in-fact ends. The son and accountant administer the trust in accordance with its terms. The terms include what happens not only if the husband dies, but also what happens to the assets while he is alive.

This is a perfect program for avoiding a costly conservatorship proceeding. But please note that it does not protect any assets from health-care or nursing-home costs for either the husband or wife.

## Concept 96

### Tests of incapacity and incompetency

Throughout these sections, I have been using the terms incapacity and incompetency. They mean different things, and you can choose the term that best meets your wishes when you delegate power over your financial affairs.

*Incompetency* is a purely legal term. It includes being unable to understand who you intend to benefit, how to handle your affairs, and how to communicate your wishes. An incompetent is stripped of his or her civil rights, like the right to vote or bring a law suit. The determination of incompetency is never taken lightly. In the famous Sonny Von Bulow case, a civil court judge held that even though the patient was in a coma, incompetency still had to be proved and, until it was, no summary judgement could be entered.

*Incapacity* is a loose term—it can be mental or physical, temporary or permanent. If you want your power of attorney to take effect if you become incapacitated, although you are not incompetent, you need a test that must be met. You can define incapacity in many ways. Here are some of the usual choices:

- the attorney-in-fact can act at his or her own discretion as to when incapacity takes place
- only when a doctor or other named or described professional gives a written opinion of incapacity
- only if the attending physician gives such a confirmation

You can also draft your own personal definition of incapacity.

## Concept 97
### Catastrophic illnesses

As medical technology becomes more advanced, it further muddies the line between life and death. Theologians, physicians and attorneys all meet to confer on what is one of the most remarkable and disturbing issues of the 20th century: When is life suuport so artificial that the living organism, although still breathing, has ceased to "be?"

While the arguments continue, the law has given ener-increasing rights to self determination. Today we are entitiled to participate in defining the moment of our own demise.

The first attempts to do so were couched in a document called a living will. A variety of nonprofit organizations fought for a patient's right to discontinue forced feeding or life support devices if they were pronounced brain dead. Many sensational law cases were part of that fight.

We've come a long way. As I write this, a doctor has just been indicted in Michigan for inventing a suicide machine. The machine has been used by two women, both with non-terminal deseases, to end their lives. A jury may find that aiding such an act is not a crime.

Today, for the most part, your options will fall into three categories. In many states you can use any of them. They are 1) the Health Care Proxy, where you delegate to another the decidion with regard to care and treatment in the event you are incompetent to decide yourself, 2) the Living Will, in which you provide the parameters within which your treating physician must operate in continuing life support treatment, 3) the Health Care Power of Attorney, virtually the same as the proxy, but it can also combine some definitive wishes on your part.

Oddly enough, all these document are drafted on behalf of those who are against the prolonged use of life support devices. The laws that support them are often called "pulling the plug" laws. If you have no such document, while there is no presumption that you *want* treatment to continue, it is likely that treatment *will* continue in the absence of a lawsuit. The cost of care and the litigation is at the family's expense. The hospital and physicians generally act as the defendants.

While this area of planning may be the most difficult, it is not necessarily an essential part of a good estate plan. The difficulty in dealing with these life and death issues should not be used as an excuse for delaying the financial aspects of planning.

To give you an idea of your drafting options, there are a number of sample approaches you can consider. Please refer to Appendix 3 for some samples of living wills.

# Things To Do

❑ Divide your assets into irrevocable, countable and non-countable lists.

❑ Research the cost of private long-term care insurance.

❑ Determine the cost of nursing homes in your area.

❑ If your level of concern is high, get referrals from your local bar association and from the Academy of Elderlaw Attorneys for a Medicaid eligibility consultation—see if trusts and/or transfers are recommended.

❑ Prepare the "power" of your choice.

# PART 7

## WHAT AND HOW TO TELL THE FAMILY ABOUT YOUR ESTATE PLAN

The last frontier of intimacy is talking about money with your parents or children. Whether you are the parent or the child, it isn't easy to sit down and talk about death and dying. But there are some things you must discuss, no matter how uncomfortable they make you or your family—what your assets are, where your assets are, and what your wishes are.

Many of us do try to talk to our children. Children often close their ears to what is said because it's too painful. Some can't face the responsibility, or are too busy. When children approach parents about the issue, the parents often back away. Perhaps they feel threatened or an invasion of privacy.

For parents who can't seem to broach the subject with children, I suggest that you put the important facts down on paper, including all the information your heirs will really need to know. Keep this document in a place accessible to your heirs. In this way, you'll assure that they'll have access to important information even if you don't discuss it with them personally.

What information should your children have? Make sure they know your full name, your legal name and any other name you might be known by. Document your marital history, your Social Security numbers, all your residential addresses, including timeshares. Children might not know that before they were born you lived in California or another community-property state. Make sure your children know your actual birthdate. If you were born in another country, make sure you still have your naturalization papers, and make them available to the kids.

Were you in the military service? Leave information about your identification number, the branch, and the unit. Are there any professional organizations that you belong to? Some of them have death benefits that you may not be aware of. Disclose the name of any professional or others that might have documents, files or information about you. Did you have prior wills or trusts that have been voided and destroyed? Let people know about all of this so there are no surprises if a document is found.

As for your present documents, you need not share the details within them during your lifetime. Trusts, wills, powers of attorney, and other documents can remain private. It is not necessary to let your family know how you are planning to distribute your assets. It *is* necessary to let them know that such estate documents exist, and where they can be found upon your death.

History of gift giving can be important. Prior to 1981, if you gave a gift of $3,000 per person or more in any given year, make a list of the donations, the date, the receiver, the type of gift, the value and whether you've ever filed a gift tax return. After 1981, do the same for any gifts of $10,000 or more.

Again, you need not reveal the gifts you have already given in your lifetime, but you should jot down those gifts and put them on your gift-giving, data-gathering page.

## Use the Financial Data Sheets in Appendix 4 to record vital information.

Once you have filled out the asset sheets, you can update them on a yearly basis to keep them as current as possible. Tell your children, "I'm not going to go through my assets with you at this moment, but I do want you to know that, together with my will or with my trust, I have updated financial data sheets. You can be aware and make our fiduciaries and professionals aware of the assets that we have."

Don't forget to share this information with your spouse. Some of you know my book ***How to Stop Fighting About Money and Make Some***, (Avon 1990). Lack of communication is one of the things that makes people fight about money. Nevertheless, maybe you have failed to let your spouse know about all your assets. Maybe your spouse has turned a deaf ear, saying "I don't want to know about these things, it's not my responsibility. You take care of the money." Now is the time to prepare the same Financial Data Sheets and tell your spouse of their existence.

## Financial information helps your heirs make the decisions you want

Very often a child named as an executor, trustee, or beneficiary comes to a crossroads in decision making after you're gone. Did Mom or Dad prefer to save estate taxes or income taxes? Would they have preferred to give money to a child or a grandchild? Was the distribution more important than the tax savings? Was there a special charity they would not want to forego? How about the family business? Did Mom or Dad want it perpetuated, or did they want it sold and the proceeds split? What about the family home or the country house?

Your heirs may be forced to make some decisions because of a failure of clarity in your will or trust. Sometimes laws intervene that you could not possibly be aware of. The family wants to know your wishes. The technical language of our wills and trusts is not always enough. Sometimes a good clear statement in plain English is helpful, not to the courts, but to the family.

So fill in the sheets at the end of this section, and pay particular attention to the section on goals and priorities. If you're speaking with your parents, ask them to set their priorities for you so that your decision-making will be easier.

# List location of documents

Once you have disclosed for your children what your assets are, you must tell them *where* they are. This is perhaps the most important part of your estate planning document survey. What documents should you have handy and where should you keep them? Keep available:

- transfer and gift tax returns
- income tax returns
- any divorce decrees
- separation decrees
- separation agreements
- prior wills
- appraisals of property
- copyrights
- royalty statements
- trust instruments
- military discharge papers
- cemetery deeds with block and lot number
- perpetual care agreements
- location of your safe deposit box
- insurance policies
- any community property.

Available does not mean in your safe deposit box in a bank or vault. Why not? Two important reasons: 1) Frequently the bank will not permit access to the safe deposit box if you are the only one whose name is listed. In some states, a marshal must be petitioned to be present for the opening of the safe deposit box, causing a lot of delay.

"What would be the harm," you may ask, "in simply putting one of my children's names on the safe deposit box so that there is joint access?" Because this could lead to questions or suspicion toward the individuals who had access to your documents.

Keep your important papers at home in a fireproof box or wall safe. The children should know the combination or, at least, where to find it.

Keep your wills and trusts with your attorney, who must relinquish those documents to your fiduciaries or your heirs if requested. This does not mean that you must force your children to use the professional that you have chosen; although it is usually wise to do so.

Almost impossible to share with your family face to face are your burial wishes. I do not support prepaid burial arrangements, except for those people who have absolutely no relatives or friends who can make those arrangements. Write your wishes out by hand and leave them with your will. Certain basic wishes can also be incorporated and included in paragraphs of the will. However, for speed, efficiency and intimacy, I suggest that you fill out the separate burial request form.

Finally, I encourage all of you to introduce your family members to your professionals. Let them meet your attorney and accountant. Inform your family members and professionals if they have been named as fiduciaries, trustees, or executors. Give them the opportunity to decline the position so that nothing unexpected happens.

## Construct a Financial Family Tree

Now, here is an important part of an estate plan that can bring the family a little closer together—"planting" the financial family tree. Have your parents shared with you the family history? Any black sheep in that closet? Well, now the time has come to find out. Create a Financial Family Tree using yourself as the client. This again makes your wishes clear and it also helps the fiduciaries, whether they're your children or the professionals your children are working with, to give notice to the proper people that may be required to receive notice under the law.

My Financial Family Tree, for example, has virtually no upper branches—as I'm not expecting to inherit from anyone and I have no brothers or sisters. The lower branches or *roots* to my tree, however, are more numerous as I plan to leave assets to my children and husband.

# Things To Do

❏ Fill out the Financial Data Sheets found in Appendix 4.

❏ Calculate your estate assets using form in Appendix 5.

❏ Decide on your beneficiaries.

❏ Decide on your fiduciaries.

❏ Introduce them to each other.

❏ Tell your beneficiaries and fiduciaries where your documents and the form you filled out are.

❏ Renew and update this form once a year, more frequently if things change radically.

# EPILOGUE

Picture two identical homes, side by side. In each live a husband, a wife and two children. Each family's income is the same, and their goals are similar.

One day, both families are visited by estate planners. In one case, the planner is a wonderful teacher and a technical genius. He spends the evening discussing every aspect of wills, trusts and insurance to the family. They feel like experts themselves. After a cup of tea, he leaves. They are happy and resolve to take action on his suggestions sometime soon.

In the other house, things are not going so well. It's hard for the planner to explain everything. The couple's minds are wandering. Besides, the planner keeps telling them to sign their will and buy insurance for the protection of the family. The planner is really annoying. After several hours, the family gives in. The will is signed, the insurance purchased. Everyone has a headache. They take an aspirin and go to bed.

The next morning, the couples leave for work. Because of their late night, they misdirect their cars while leaving their adjoining driveways. They collide and are instantly killed.

Which of the children are better off?

This book and any like it is no substitute to taking action. All the book learning in the world will not put money in your family's pocket. It did not put any into ours when my attorney/CPA/father died suddenly at age 44 with no plan and no insurance.

Enough said.

# APPENDIX 1

# GLOSSARY

**Accumulation of assets:** Leaving the growth or income from a trust fund in the trust without distributing it to beneficiaries, usually a power of the trustee. Often used when beneficiaries are minors.

**Administration of estates:** Supervision of a decedent's estate by an executor or administrator.

**Administrator:** One given authority to settle the estate of a decedent who dies without a will.

**Alimony:** Support and maintenance either pursuant to a court order of divorce or voluntary separation agreement. It is not taxable as income to the receiving spouse or deductible by the paying spouse.

**Antenuptial/prenuptial agreement:** A document signed before or during marriage agreeing to the distribution of assets in the event of a divorce or death. Sometimes also agrees to the handling of income and assets during a marriage.

**Attestation clause:** The closing of a will that is signed by the testator (will maker) acknowledged and witnessed.

**Attorney-in-fact:** A person who is given the power to act on another's behalf by virtue of a signed document called a power of attorney. Can be a limited power to do only one act, or a general power to act with discretion on all matters on another's behalf.

**Basis:** The original purchase price paid for property, plus the cost of improvements, attorney's fees and other costs of purchase and sale. Basis is deducted from sale price to determine the profit made when the assets are sold. The profit will be subject to a capital gains tax.

**Beneficiary:** individuals you wish to get the benefit of your assets, whether you will to them or establish trusts that provide them with income or principal.

**Bequest or Legacy:** A gift of personal property made in a will; a gift of real property made in a will.

**Capital gains tax:** The tax on the profit made from the sale of an asset. At present, capped at 28 percent.

**Chancery court:** Also called surrogate's court. The court with jurisdiction to hear wills, trusts and estate cases.

**Charitable trust:** A trust naming a charity as beneficiary of income or principal.

**Codicil:** A written addition or amendment to a will.

**Common interest:** A shared interest among many people or entities in real estate. The owners of a condominium have a common interest in the community pool.

**Conservatorship:** A formal proceeding in which the court appoints another person to act on behalf of another in business and/or personal matters.

**Constructive trust:** A trust imposed by a court pursuant to court order stating that a person is in charge of an asset for the benefit of another even though there is no trust document. Usually done to protect someone whose property is wrongfully held by someone else, and should have been in their name in the first place.

**Contingent beneficiary:** One entitled to profit from a contract or estate only upon the occurrence of a specified event, usually one who receives assets at the death of the primary or lifetime beneficiary.

**Corpus:** Money, bonds, stocks, diamonds or whatever else you wish to give to the trustee for the benefit of the beneficiary.

**Countable assets:** Assets that will be counted to determine if an individual is eligible for Medicaid.

**Credit shelter clause:** Called *Superclause* in this book. A clause in a will or trust used by married couples to preserve the estate tax exclusion, which is usually wasted if one spouse leaves everything to the other outright. The use of the clause saves as much as $192,800 in taxes and requires the surviving spouse to receive income only from assets when the first spouse dies.

**Crummey power:** The power of a beneficiary to receive certain assets from a trust immediately so that it is not considered a future gift and can qualify for certain tax exclusion.

**Decedent:** A deceased person.

**Demonstrative Bequest or Legacy:** A gift of property to be taken out of a larger holding of specific identified property.

**Descendants:** Persons who follow decedent in line of descent.

**Devisee:** One who gets a gift of real property in a will.

**Disclaimer:** Formal refusal to accept an inheritance, must be made within 9 months of death and filed on an Internal Revenue form. The purpose is to engage in post mortem tax planning, and is most often used when a will does not contain a Superclause and the spouse decides to disclaim all or part of the inheritance in favor of the children so as not to waste the decedents estate tax credit (also called a renunciation).

**Distribution of assets:** The act of a trustee in paying out assets to beneficiaries.

**Durable power of attorney:** A power of attorney that stays in effect even after the maker of the power becomes incompetent.

**Dynasty trust:** A name given by the author to describe a trust that lasts through several generations, allowing the maker of the trust to use the assets under certain circumstances. Usually funded with insurance.

**Elective share:** The right of a surviving spouse of a valid marriage to get a portion of the deceased spouse's estate. Most states require one-third of the estate go to the spouse even if the decedent tried to disinherit the spouse.

**Escheat:** The right of the state to succeed to property, either real or personal where there is no heir.

**Estate tax:** Inheritance tax.

**Estate:** The assets and liabilities, real and personal property, left by a decedent.

**Executor:** The fiduciary named in a will who distributes the assets and closes the estate. The executor is personally liable if estate taxes are not paid.

**Failure of issue:** To die without lineal descendants.

**Federal exemption:** $600,000 in assets is exempt from federal estate taxes. This translates to a tax credit of $192,800.

**Fee simple absolute:** A way of owning real estate in which the owner has full title and can sell, mortgage, transfer or do any other legal act with respect to the real estate. It is the way most of us own our homes.

**Fiduciary:** A trusted representative, an executor or trustee, must exercise the responsibility with prudence.

**General bequest or legacy:** A gift that isn't specific, usually a sum of money.

**Generation-skipping trusts:** A trust in which the one who sets up the trust and the beneficiary are a generation apart. For example, grandparents can set up a generation-skipping trust for grandchildren.

**Gift tax:** Tax levied on gifts of property, to supplement estate and inheritance tax.

**GRAT:** Grantor Retained Annuity Trust. A trust in which the grantor (the one who sets up the trust) gets an annuity for life.

**GRIT:** Grantor Retained Interest Trust. A trust in which the grantor has an interest in the assets.

**GRUT:** Grantor Retained Unit Trust. A trust in which the grantor retains an income based on the performance of the assets in the trust.

**Guardian *ad litem*:** A person appointed by the court to oversee the appointment of a conservator, an individual to handle an incompetent's assets, and to determine whether the individual is really incompetent.

**Health care power of attorney:** A power of attorney that allows the holder to decide on the care of an incompetent person.

**Health care proxy:** Same as *health care power of attorney*. Usually relates only to life support care.

**Heir testamentary:** One to whom property is left by will.

**Heir:** One who inherits property.

**Inaccessible assets:** An asset that is not counted in determining Medicaid eligibility, because it is not accessible to the applicant.

**Inchoate interest:** An interest that has not vested; a mere expectancy to receive an interest in an estate at some future time.

**Income:** Value earned by principal assets.

**Incompetency:** The state of being declared legally incapable of handling assets and exercising certain legal rights.

*In Terrorem:* A clause under which an individual is disinherited. If the individual wages a contest, he or she will forfeit any share even if the will is invalidated.

*Inter vivos* **trusts:** Also known as "living" trusts, these are trusts that you create during your lifetime. You can even be the trustee. The trust can terminate on your death or during your own lifetime. One that you create during your lifetime can pour over into another trust in your will so that it continues even after your death.

**Intestate:** One who dies without a will.

**Invasion of principal:** The power of a trustee to take assets of a trust and distribute them to a beneficiary.

**Irrevocable trust:** A trust in which an interest is given to another, and in which the settlor retains no incidents of ownership or control.

**Issue:** Lineal descendants.

**Joint tenancy:** A holding of property by several persons in such a way that any one of them can act as owner of the whole and take the property by survivorship.

**Joint-and-survivor insurance:** A policy underwritten on the life of two persons; either husband and wife or business partners.

**Kiddie tax:** A tax on the income of children under the age of 14 based on their parents' marginal tax bracket.

**Kin:** Related by blood or legal ties.

**Last will and testament:** An instrument whereby one makes a disposition of his property to take effect after his death.

**Lease hold:** The right to occupy but not own real estate.

**Legatee:** One who gets a gift of personal property in a will.

**Letters testamentary:** Letters issued by a court empowering an executor of a will to act.

**Letter precatory:** A private letter to a fiduciary stating how art, antiques, jewelry and other tangibles are to be distributed. It is written by the testator and left with the will or other important papers.

**Life estate:** The right to occupy, rent out, use property for life, no right to sell or otherwise dispose of the property as it is being held for another who will receive it upon the life tenants death. The life tenant is a fiduciary of the eventual owner with respect to that property.

**Life insurance trust:** A trust created solely for the purpose of owning life insurance policies; usually an irrevocable trust.

**Life interest:** An interest in property, which is to terminate upon the death of the holder of the interest or some other designated person.

**Life tenancy:** The right to occupy real estate for life. The life tenant can rent the property and keep the rent and hold it as a fiduciary for the eventual beneficiary.

**Lineal descendants:** Individuals related by blood, following a line of descent from generation to generation.

**Living trusts:** Trusts that are made and take effect during the trustors lifetime. They can be revocable or irrevocable. Also called *inter vivos* trusts. One popular trust is the probate-avoiding revocable trust.

**Living will:** A document that formally and, in some states legally expresses your wish to forgo extraordinary medical treatment when you become terminally ill.

**Marital deduction:** Exempts from estate tax all property passing from one spouse to the other by reason of gift or death (IRC section 2056).

**Medicaid:** A program of the federal government in which the states provide health care for the poor.

**Medicare:** A program of the federal government providing health care for seniors and certain disabled persons. It does not provide for long-term care of the elderly except under limited conditions and has resulted in many middle-class elderly becoming impoverished and Medicaid-eligible.

***Per stirpes*:** By legal definition, the term refers to your children downward (your children, grandchildren, great-grandchildren, and so on).

***Per capita*:** People of the same degree of kinship, such as all of your children or all of your nieces and nephews.

**Perfect trust:** Executed trust; signed by the settlor(s).

**Personal property clause:** Wills or trust clauses to cover your books, jewelry, art. clothing and other tangibles.

**Pour over will:** Instrument that provides that property not previously transferred into a revocable living trust is to be transferred at the death of the settlor.

**Power of attorney:** Document appointing someone to act in your place. (See *durable power of attorney*.)

**Present interest:** A present right and ownership to an asset. A gift not contingent on a specific event.

**Principal:** Asset of value which may earn income. Also called *corpus*.

**Probate:** The process of proving a will is valid.

**Probate court:** Court established for the administration of the estates of decedents, and the control of the adoption and guardianship of minors.

**QTIP trust:** Qualified Terminable Interest trust in which all income is payable to the surviving spouse at least annually and which qualifies for the marital deduction. (IRC section 2056).

**Real property:** Land.

**Realty:** Land or real property.

**Receiver:** One appointed to hold in trust property under litigation.

**Remainder interest:** Interest in the principal of a trust after the income beneficiary has died, or upon another event that terminates the trust.

**Remainder:** Property or principal that remains after the trust is terminated.

**Remaindermen:** Persons designated to receive property following the initial distribution of the estate.

**Residuary Bequest or Legacy:** A gift of the balance of all your property after payment of taxes, debts, expenses and specific, demonstrative, or general bequests or legacies.

**Revocable trust:** A trust in which a contingent interest is given to another and in which the settlor retains a present interest, ownership, and control.

**Revocation clause:** The clause that revokes all prior wills and codicils when you make a new will.

**Right of courtesy:** Marital property rights that women are entitled to by law from their husbands.

**Right of dower:** Marital property rights that men are entitled to by law from their wives.

**Second-to-die:** A type of insurance policy for couples and business partners. (See *joint-and-survivor insurance*.)

**Self proving:** A type of will with a special clause that makes it unnecessary to bring in the witnesses at the time of probate.

**Sensitive trustee:** A trustee or successor trustee who is also a beneficiary.

**Settlor/grantor:** the person who creates the trust.

**Simultaneous death clause:** A directive in a will or trust as to whom should be presumed to have died first if the testator and a beneficiary die in a common disaster.

**Specific Bequest or Legacy:** A gift of an identified item.

**Spendthrift clause:** A clause in a trust that makes the trust *corpus* untouchable by creditors of the beneficiary.

**Spousal Impoverishment Act:** A federal statute determining the use of assets of the healthy spouse to support the spouse who requires long-term care.

**Sprinkling trust:** A trust with more than one beneficiary in which the trustee has the power to distribute assets and income in different amounts to different beneficiaries as circumstances require. Most often used when beneficiaries are in a state of flux. For example, going to college, in financial difficulty, etc.

**Stepped-up basis:** Tax rule that gives a person who inherits property a more attractive basis, figured on the value of the property at the time of the owner's death or six months afterward. Because the value of the property is generally greater than it was at time of purchase, this lowers the difference between the selling price and the value plus costs, which results in lower taxes assessed.

**Succession:** The taking of property by inheritance or will or by operation of law.

**Successor trustee:** Individual who succeeds to the power to manage trust assets.

**Superclause:** The author's name for a credit shelter clause. A clause in a will or trust used by married couples to preserve the estate tax exclusion, which is usually wasted if one spouse leaves everything to the other outright. The use of the clause saves as much as $192,800 in taxes and requires the surviving spouse to receive income only from assets when the first spouse dies.

**Surrogate's court:** The judge in this courts is a substitute for the deceased.

**Tax and debt clause:** A clause in a will or trust empowering the fiduciary to pay debts and taxes, selecting the assets from which they are to be paid.

**Tenancy in common:** Tenancy in lands by more than one person in such a way that each owns an undivided share.

**Testamentary trusts:** These trusts are created in your will or in an *inter vivos* trust, and come into action upon your death.

**Testate:** One who has made a will or dies leaving a will.

**Testator:** An individual who dies leaving a valid will.

**Trust:** A written document designed to put your money in the hands of a third party, so that the third party can use it *only* for the benefit of your designated loved one.

**Trustee:** One appointed to manage a trust.

**Trustor:** One who settles or creates a trust; the grantor.

**Unfunded trust:** A trust that holds no assets. Often a sprinkling power of attorney is used to give the power to fund a trust when the settlor becomes incompetent so that his or her assets can be handled in accordance with the trust provisions.

**Unified credit:** The total amount of gifts and inheritance excluded from federal estate tax. Currently, this is $600,000. ($1.2 million for a married couple.)

**Uniform Gifts to Minors Act:** A statute enacted in all states to permit assets to be given to minors. The income is taxed at the minor's income rate and it can still be controlled by the donor until the minor turns 21.

**Unity of title:** That essential aspect of joint tenancy, that the estates of the joint tenants be created by one and the same act.

**Vested:** An unconditional right to or interest in property.

**Will:** Statement indicating an individual's desires as to the distribution of wealth following his or her death.

# SAMPLE WILLS AND TESTAMENTARY INSTRUMENTS

## 1. An Annotated Will for Drafting With 10 Drafter's Comments

The following is an actual will of a New Jersey couple with two children. The will was drafted after data gathering and discussion. With every first-time will presentation, an annexed annotation sheet should be given to the client, who will resolve ambiguities in the mind of the drafter. A standard sheet follows; for many wills, additional comments can be included at the bottom of the form.

### Questions for client to answer to eliminate ambiguities

1. Is there any other name used by the testator?
2. Are there other domiciles or significant property outside the domicile belonging to the testator?
3. Is there an existing will or codicil?
4. Is there a former spouse?
5. Are there any adopted, out-of-wedlock or yet unknown children?
6. Are there any special burial instructions?
7. Are there any specific debts or expenses already contemplated?
8. Would the testator rather have taxes taken from a specific fund or legacy?

9. Does the testator wish a different distribution, i.e., a trust for the personal property or a letter precatory?

10. Does the testator wish a marital trust or a Super-clause?

11. How does testator wish to provide for minors?

12. A vast variety of residuary bequests are possible. Are your wishes expressed?

13. If a corporate co-executor or trustee is named, does he or she require any specific clauses; do you wish to restrict the corporate co-executor or trustee in any way?

14. Do you wish statements regarding compensation or posting of bond or liability by fiduciaries?

15. Long-form powers are more appropriate if assets are complex.

16. Check consequences (usually tax consequences) of the simultaneous death clause.

17. Are there any natural parents that can contest a designation of guardianship?

18. Be sure name is same throughout document.

# Long Form Annotated Will

I, [ ], of the City, County and State of declare this to be my last will and testament.

**I.**

I revoke all my prior wills and codicils.

**II.**

I give all my tangible personal property to my wife, if she survives me, together with all insurance policies thereon, if any. If my wife does not survive me, I give such property to those of my children who survive me, in approximately equal shares, as my Executors in their exclusive discretion shall determine.

> **\*\*1.** Together with any tangible personal property so that the new owner can take over existing policies and take advantage of the already paid premiums.
>
> **\*\*2.** This clause gives great discretion to the Executor to divide shares and is usually best done with a family member as Executor.

**III.**

I give all the rest of my property, hereinafter referred to as "my residuary estate," to my wife, [ ], if she survives me. If my wife does not survive me, my residuary estate shall be disposed of as provided in article **IV** if I have issue surviving me, or as provided in article **V** if I have no such issue.

> **\*\*3.** This residuary clause gives everything to the spouse. In a more affluent estate, the drafter would use a Credit Shelter Trust to preserve federal and state exemptions.
>
> **\*\*4.** This is an outright gift, which qualifies for the marital deduction for federal estate tax purposes and for tax purposes in many states. In a more affluent estate the same purposes could be achieved through a trust called the QTIP or Credit Shelter Trust.

**5. In the event that the spouse predeceases, surviving children will be provided for and if there aren't any, then family members will receive the bequests. This is most usual with a young couple who do not yet have grandchildren and may not yet have children.

## IV.

If my wife, [    ], does not survive me, but I have issue surviving me, my Executors shall divide my residuary estate into as many equal shares as will permit them to set apart one such share for each child of mine who survives me and one such share for the issue surviving me of each child of mine who fails to survive me but leaves such issue, and I dispose of such shares as follows:

(a)    I give one such share to the issue surviving me of each child of mine who fails to survive me but leaves such issue.

(b)    I give one such share to each child of mine who survives me and has attained the age of thirty-five at the time of my death.

(c)    I give each share which is set apart from a child of mine who survives me but has not attained the age of thirty-five years at the time of my death ("the beneficiary") to my Trustees, termination of the trust, for the following purposes:

(1)    During the minority of the beneficiary, in the sole discretion of my Trustees, to pay any part or all of the income to, or to accumulate any part or all of the income for the benefit of the beneficiary. Any income not so paid or accumulated shall be added to the principal of the trust.

(2)    After the beneficiary who has attained the age of twenty-one years, to pay the income to him or her in convenient installments at least quarter-annually.

(3)     To pay to the beneficiary at any time or times prior to their termination of the trust, such sums from or any part or all of the principal as my Trustees may, in their sole discretion, determine to be reasonably necessary to permit the beneficiary to maintain his or her usual standard of living, including the costs of his or her undergraduate or post-graduate education, and the expenses of any illness or accident which may affect him or her.

(4)     To pay to the beneficiary, upon his or her attaining the age of twenty-five years, a sum from or part of the property which then constitutes the principal of the trust equivalent in value to one-third of such principal; upon his or her attaining the age of thirty years, a sum from or part of the property which then constitutes the principal of the trust equivalent in value to one-third of such principal, and to pay to the beneficiary upon his or her attaining the age of thirty-five years, the entire principal, if any, remaining at that time.

If the beneficiary has attained the age of twenty-five or thirty years prior to his or her share being set apart, then when such share is set apart for his or her benefit, my Trustees shall distribute to him or her one-third or two-thirds of the value thereof, as the case may be.

(5)     Upon the death of the beneficiary prior to his or her thirty-fifth birthday, to pay the then remaining principal, if any, to his or her then living issue, or if he or she has no such issue, to my then living issue, except that any share which would be payable to a child of mine who is then under the age of thirty-five years shall instead be added to the principal of

the trust created under this subarticle (c) of article **IV** for the primary benefit of such child. If I also have no issue then living, such principal shall be disposed of as provided in article **V**.

> **6. The residuary estate, in the event the spouse is predeceased, is divided up into equal shares for each child or each grandchild if a child has predeceased the Testator. Each child of age thirty-five is given his or her share outright. Anyone under the age of thirty-five, becomes the beneficiary of a Trust to last until the child reaches thirty-five. Prior to that time the child will receive income from the Trust at the discretion of the Trustee beginning at age twenty-one. The Trustee also has the discretion to invade the Trust for certain purposes such as college and medical help. One-third of the principal of the Trust is paid over to the beneficiary at age twenty-five and again a sum at age thirty. If the beneficiary does not reach the age thirty-five when they would be entitled to an outright gift, then his or her share is added to the principal for the benefit of the qualifying beneficiaries.

**V.**

Any property which I have directed to be disposed of as provided in this article shall be divided into two equal parts, which I dispose of as follows:

(a)    I give one such part to my mother, [   ], if she is then living. If my mother is not then living, or if she disclaims all or a portion of her part, then I give this part, or the disclaimed portion thereof, to the then living issue of my parents, [   ] and [   ], in equal shares.

(b)    I give the other such part, in equal shares, to my mother-in-law, [   ], and my father-in-law, [   ], if they are both then living, or if only one of them is then living, all to the survivor. If neither my mother-in-law nor my father-in-law is then living, or if one or both of them disclaim all or a portion thereof, to the then living issue of my mother-in-law and my father-in-law, [ ] and [ ], in equal shares.

**7. Such tailored trusts require substantial administration and are best included when there is a professional trustee who is willing to handle the estate because of its size or where there is devoted family member trustee who is fully aware of the terms of the trust and the intent of the Testator. These clauses will take place only under the remote circumstances that the Testator is survived by no spouse, child or grandchild. These clauses are traditional, general bequests. Note in 5 (a) the reference to disclaimer. This dictates who shall receive any disclaimed inheritance. Since the beneficiary is Testator's mother, if the mother is elderly or frail, she may not wish to take her inheritance but pass it to a younger beneficiary. If so, the testator has named the beneficiary and therefore controls the descent. Without so naming, the bequests would go to the next of kin under the applicable state statute.

## VI.

If, under the terms of other provisions of this will, any money or other property is required to be distributed to a person who is a minor or who is otherwise under a disability (such as incompetency), I direct that such money or other property not be distributed, but that instead it be held by my Trustees, IN TRUST, for the following purposes:

(a)     During the period of minority or other disability, the Trustees shall pay to the minor or other person under a disability any part or all of the income or principal as the Trustees may, in their discretion, determine to be reasonably necessary for such person's support, maintenance, education, or health or to meet the costs of any illness or accident affecting such person.

(b)     During the period of minority or other disability, the Trustees may accumulate any part of the income not disposed of pursuant to subarticle (a) of this article, or they may add such income to principal.

(c)     Upon the termination of minority or the other disability, the Trustees shall pay all remaining property to the person whose minority or disability has terminated, or in the event such person has died before attaining majority or without termination of the disability, the Trustees shall distribute such property to such person's estate.

> **8. This is a catch-all clause providing for minors who may be beneficiaries, who are not included in the residuary minors trust. Frequently, the client questions this clause, if there are no minors who are not already provided for. It is suggested that the clause be included with an explanation that it is merely for the protection of remote beneficiaries. It is also to be noted that the clause pertains in the event of a disability such as mental incompetency, which might be applicable in the case of an elderly spouse.

## VII.

Any property which my Trustees are authorized to pay to a person who is a minor or otherwise under a disability, may, in the discretion of my Trustee, be paid for the benefit of such person to a guardian or to another individual who is not under a disability with whom the minor or otherwise disabled person resides. If my Trustees obtain a receipt for any payment made in accordance with this provision, such receipt shall fully discharge them from liability with respect to such payment and from further accountability therefor.

> **9. See 8 above.

## VIII.

Whenever my Trustees are directed or authorized to make payments to a person, my Trustees are authorized, in their discretion, to apply such payments to or for the use of such person.

## IX.

The word "issue" as used in this will shall mean issue *per stirpes*, and shall include those born after my death. The word "minor," as used in this will shall mean a person who has not attained the age of twenty-one years. The use of the masculine shall include the feminine, the feminine shall include the masculine, and the use of the singular and the plural shall be interchangeable.

## X.

I direct that all estate, inheritance and other death taxes (including any interest thereon and penalties with respect thereto), federal, state and other, imposed by reason of my death in respect of property passing under this will or otherwise, shall be paid out of my residuary estate.

## XI.

If my wife, [   ], and I should die under such circumstances that it cannot be determined which of us died first, my wife shall be deemed to have survived me.

\*\*10. Refer to Chapter 1, Concept 19, for analysis of the simultaneous death clauses.

## XII.

If my wife, [  ], does not survive me, I appoint my sister, as guardian of the person and property of each of my children during his or her minority. If my sister, for any reason, fails to qualify or ceases to act as guardian, I appoint my sister-in-law, [  ], and my brother-in-law, [  ], or the survivor of them, as guardians in her place. No one acting as guardian shall be required to furnish any bond or security of any kind for the faithful performance of his or her duties as guardian.

## XIII.

I appoint my wife, [   ], as Executor of this will. If she, for any reason, fails to qualify or at any time ceases to act as Executor, I appoint my sister, [   ], and my brother-in-law, [   ], as Executors in her place.

I appoint my sister, [   ], and my brother-in-law, [   ], as Trustees of the trusts created herein.

If the number of Trustees acting hereunder is at any time reduced to one, I authorize such last acting Trustee to appoint either a co-Trustee or a successor Trustee. Any such appointment shall be made by a written instrument filed with the Court in which my will is admitted to probate.

Any reference in this will to my Executor or Trustees shall be deemed to refer to successors, survivors and co-Trustees appointed as above authorized.

No one acting as Executor or Trustee shall be required to furnish any bond or security of any kind for the faithful performance of his or her duties as Executor of Trustee.

## XIV.

In addition to the powers conferred by law or by other provisions of this will upon my Executor and my Trustees, I direct that they shall have the following discretionary powers:

(1)     To retain any property which I may own at the time of my death or which may at any time be in their hands, or to sell, exchange or otherwise dispose of any such property, at

public or private sale, without application to court, on any terms, including the extension of credit, which they deem advisable.

(2) To acquire, by purchase or otherwise, any property, real or personal, without being limited by any provision of law which restricts investments by fiduciaries and without regard to any principles of diversification, including but not limited to common and preferred stocks, bonds, common trust funds, secured and unsecured obligations and mortgages.

(3) To acquire and pay for, exercise, or sell any options or subscription rights in connection with securities or any other property.

(4) To hold securities in the names of nominees or in bearer form.

(5) To operate, repair, alter, improve, insure, grant options upon, mortgage partition, or lease for any period of time any real property or interest in real property which at any time forms part of my estate or of any trust herein created.

(6) To retain and pay, as an expense of administration, accountants, attorneys, bookkeepers, investments advisors, stenographers, and other assistants.

(7) To borrow money from any source and for any purpose, including but not limited to the payment of taxes, and to pledge or mortgage any assets of my estate of any trust created hereunder as security for money borrowed.

(8) To pay any gift and to make distributions of my estate or from any trust created hereunder in cash or in kind, or

partly in each, and to allocate property to any gift or trust other than ratably.

(9)     To hold property of separate trusts in common investments for convenience or investment or administration.

(10)     To determine whether to claim deductions available to me or to my estate on estate tax or on income tax returns, and to determine whether to use date of death or alternate valuation date values for estate tax purposes, in such manner as they consider advisable and with or without making any adjustments between income and principal or among beneficiaries due to any such determinations, as they, in their discretion, decide.

(11)     To determine whether or not to consent to an election by any corporation to be taxed under Subchapter S of the Internal Revenue Code of 1954, as amended.

(12)     To continue any business in which I have an interest for any period of time which the consider advisable, or to sell or otherwise dispose of any such business.

(13)     Whenever more than one Executor or Trustee has been appointed and is acting as such, to delegate to any one of my Executors or Trustees any nondiscretionary power, including but not limited to the power to sign checks and bank withdrawal slips and the power to have access to safe deposit boxes in which property belonging to my estate or to any trust created hereunder is being held.

My Trustees shall continue to have all the rights, powers and duties herein vested in them after the termination or any trust created hereunder and until the complete distribution of all property held by them.

IN WITNESS WHEREOF, I have hereunto set my hand and seal this _____ day of _____, one thousand nine hundred and eighty-seven (1987).

_____ L.S.(Legal Signature)

## 2. Last Will and Testament

I, PETER PAUL, a resident of and domiciled in the State of New York, make, publish and declare this to be my Last Will and Testament, revoking my prior wills and codicils.

**I.**

My wife's name is MARY PAUL, and I presently have one child, PAUL PAUL.

**II.**

I direct that the expenses of my last illness and funeral, and the expenses of the administration of my estate, and all estate, inheritance, legacy, transfer, succession and similar death taxes and duties, and any interest or penalties thereon, payable with respect to property included in my taxable estate (whether or not passing under this will), shall be paid out of the principal of my estate as an expense of administration, without apportionment.

**III.**

I give all my personal effects and belongings, household furniture and furnishings, clothing, books, automobiles and all other tangible personal property (except cash and currency), to my wife, MARY PAUL, or if she shall not survive me, to my then living children, in equal shares, to be divided among them as they shall agree upon, or if they shall be unable to agree upon such division, as my Executor shall determine.

**IV.**

I give all the rest, residue and remainder of my property, both real and personal, of whatsoever kind and nature and wherever located (hereinafter referred to as my "residuary estate"), to which I shall be entitled in any manner at the time of my death, as follows:

(a) If my wife MARY PAUL shall survive me, to my wife outright.

(b) If my wife shall not survive me, then to those of my children who survive me and to the issue who survive me of those of my children who predecease me, *per stirpes*.

(c) If my wife shall not survive me and there shall be no issue of mine then living, I give my residuary estate to those who would take from me as if I were then to die intestate, unmarried, the absolute owner of my residuary estate, and a resident of the State of New York.

## V.

If upon my death any property would vest in a person who is a minor or incompetent, then my Executor may pay or distribute the whole or any part of such property to such beneficiary; or may apply the whole or any part of such property directly to the care, comfort, support, maintenance, education and welfare of such beneficiary; or may pay or distribute the whole or any part of such property to the guardian, committee, conservator or other legal representative, wherever appointed, of such beneficiary, or to the person with whom such beneficiary resides, or, in case such beneficiary shall be a minor, to a custodian for such minor under the gifts to minors act selected by my Executor, the receipt of the person to whom any such payment or distribution is so made being a sufficient discharge therefore even though my Executor may be such person; or may defer payment or distribution of the whole or any part of the property to which a minor may be entitled until such minor shall attain the age of eighteen (18) years, and hold the whole or the undistributed portion thereof as a separate fund for such minor absolutely and with all of the powers and authority set forth in Article **VII** hereof; or may accumulate and invest the whole or any part of the property to which a minor may be entitled for the benefit of such minor and pay, distribute or apply any such property or income therefrom to or for the benefit of such minor as provided above at any time during minority, and pay over any balance thereof to such minor when such minor shall attain the age of eighteen (18) years or, in case such minor shall die before attaining said age, to the executor, administrator or other legal representative of the estate of such minor or if there shall be no such legal representative, to such persons as would have taken if such minor died intestate, unmarried, the absolute owner thereof and a resident of the state in which such minor shall die domiciled. For purposes hereof, a "minor" shall mean any person who has not attained the age of eighteen (18) years.

## VI.

I appoint my wife, MARY PAUL, to be my Executor. I direct that no Executor acting hereunder shall be required to file or furnish any bond or other security for the faithful performance of the duties of my Executor as such, notwithstanding any provision of the law to the contrary.

**VII.**

I hereby grant to my Executor all powers conferred on executors by Article 11 of the Estates, Powers and Trusts Law of the State of New York, as amended and in effect from time to time, and all of the powers conferred by law upon executors in any jurisdiction in which my Executor may act. without limiting any other powers granted by this will or by law, I give to my Executor power to retain, sell at public or private sale, exchange, grant options on, invest and reinvest in (without limitation to so-called "legal investments"), or otherwise deal with property of any nature upon terms and for cash or upon credit; to compromise, modify and release claims with or without consideration; to execute and deliver instruments, including releases which shall constitute a complete discharge for any property or claim embraced therein; to employ legal and investment counsel, custodians, accountants and agents for the transaction of any business of my estate or for services or advice; to make division or distribution in cash or in kind or partly in each; and to exercise in good faith and reasonable care all other investment and administrative powers and discretions of an absolute owner which lawfully may be conferred upon a fiduciary.

**VIII.**

In the event that any beneficiary under this will and I shall die in a common accident or disaster or under circumstances in which it is difficult or impractical to determine who survived the other, then for the purposes of this will such beneficiary shall be deemed to have predeceased me. The words "child" and "children," wherever used in this will, shall include not only the natural child and children (whether heretofore or hereafter born) of the person or persons designated, but also the legally adopted child and children of such person or persons. The word "issue," wherever used in this will shall include not only the natural child, children and issue (whether heretofore or hereafter born) of the person or persons designated, but also the legally adopted child and children of such person or persons and of the child, children or issue thereof. Wherever use in this will and the context so requires, the masculine shall include the feminine and the singular shall include the plural, and vice versa.

**IX.**

If my wife shall not survive me, I appoint my sister PAULA PAUL to be guardian of the person and property of each child of mine who has not attained the age of eighteen (18) years. I direct that no guardian herein named shall be required to file or furnish any bond or other security for the faithful performance of his duties as guardian, notwithstanding any provision of the law to the contrary.

IN WITNESS WHEREOF, I, PETER PAUL, have hereunto set my hand and seal this _____ day of _____, 1987.

_____(L.S.)

The foregoing instrument was signed, sealed, published and declared by PETER PAUL, the above named Testator, as and for his Last Will and Testament, in our presence, all being present at the same time, thereupon we, at his request and in his presence and in the presence of each other, have hereunto subscribed our names as witnesses.

_____  residing at

_____

_____  residing at

_____

_____  residing at

_____

# APPENDIX 3

# SAMPLE LIVING WILLS

### [SAMPLE]*

### "LIVING WILL"

#### DECLARATION

Declaration made this _____ day of
_____ 198___ .

I, _____ ,
being of sound mind, willfully and voluntarily make
known my desires that my dying shall not be artificially prolonged under the circumstances set forth
below, and do declare:

If at any time I should have an incurable injury,
disease, or illness certified to be a terminal condition
by two (2) physicians who have personally examined
me, one of whom shall be my attending physician, and
the physicians have determined that my death will
occur whether or not life-sustaining procedures are
utilized and where the application of life-sustaining
procedures would serve only to artificially prolong
the dying process, I direct that such procedures be
withheld or withdrawn, and that I be permitted to die
naturally with only the administration of medication
or the performance of any medical procedure deemed
necessary to provide me with comfort, care or to
alleviate pain.

In the absence of my ability to give directions
regarding the use of such life-sustaining procedures, it
is my intention that this declaration shall be honored
by my family and physician(s) as the final expression
of my legal right to refuse medical or surgical treatment and accept the consequences from such refusal.

I understand the full import of this declaration and
I am emotionally and mentally competent to make
this declaration.

Signed _____

Address_____

_____

I believe the declarant to be of sound mind. I did not
sign the declarant's signature above for or at the direc-
tion of the declarant. I am at least 18-years of age and
am not related to the declarant by blood or marriage,

entitled to any portion of the estate of the declarant
according to the laws of intestate succession of the
_____ or under any
will of the declarant or codicil thereto, or directly
financially responsible for declarant's medical care.
I am not the declarant's attending physician, an
employee of the attending physician, or an employee
of the health facility in which the declarant is a
patient.

Witness_____

Address_____

_____

Witness_____

Address_____

_____

ss.:

Before me, the undersigned authority, on this
_____ day of_____ ,
198___, personally appeared _____ ,
_____ , and
_____ , known
to me to be the Declarant and the witnesses, respec-
tively, whose names are signed to the foregoing instrument, and who, in the presence of each other, did
subscribe their names to the attached Declaration
(Living Will) on this date, and that said Declarant at
the time of execution of said Declaration was over the
age of eighteen (18) years and of sound mind.

[SEAL]
My commission expires:

_____
Notary Public

*Check requirements of individual state statute.

Source: President's Commission for the Study of Ethical Problems in Medicine and Biobehavioral Research, "Deciding To Forego Life-Sustaining Treatment," U.S. Government Printing Office, pages 314–315.

191

## DURABLE POWER OF ATTORNEY
## FOR HEALTH CARE

I, _____

hereby appoint:

_____
name

_____
home address

_____

_____

_____
home telephone number

_____
work telephone number

as my agent to make health care decisions for me if and when I am unable to make my own health care decisions. This gives my agent the power to consent to giving, withholding or stopping any health care, treatment, service, or diagnostic procedure. My agent also has the authority to talk with health care personnel, get information, and sign forms necessary to carry out those decisions.

If the person named as my agent is not available or is unable to act as my agent, then I appoint the following person(s) to serve in the order listed below:

1. _____
   name

   _____
   home address

   _____

   _____

   _____
   home telephone number

   _____
   work telephone number

2. _____
   name

   _____
   home address

   _____

   _____

   _____
   home telephone number

   _____
   work telephone number

*Check requirements of individual state statute.
Source: Barbara Mishkin, Hogan and Hartson.

By this document I intend to create a power of attorney for health care which shall take effect upon my incapacity to make my own health care decisions and shall continue during that incapacity.

My agent shall make health care decisions as I direct below or as I make known to him or her in some other way.

(a) STATEMENT OF DESIRES CONCERNING LIFE-PROLONGING CARE, TREATMENT, SERVICES, AND PROCEDURES:

_____

_____

_____

_____

_____

_____

_____

(b) SPECIAL PROVISIONS AND LIMITATIONS:

_____

_____

_____

_____

_____

_____

_____

_____

_____

_____

(Continued)

**BY SIGNING HERE I INDICATE THAT I UN-DERSTAND THE PURPOSE AND EFFECT OF THIS DOCUMENT.**

I sign my name to this form on_____ .
(date)

My current home address: _____

_____

_____
(You sign here)

## WITNESSES

I declare that the person who signed or ac-knowledged this document is personally known to me, that he/she signed or acknowledged this durable power of attorney in my presence, and that he/she appears to be of sound mind and under no duress, fraud, or undue influence. I am not the person appointed as agent by this document, nor am I the patient's health care provider, or an employee of the patient's health care provider.

**First Witness**

Signature: _____

Home Address: _____

Print Name: _____

Date:_____

**Second Witness**

Signature: _____

Home Address: _____

Print Name: _____

Date:_____

(AT LEAST ONE OF THE ABOVE WITNESSES MUST ALSO SIGN THE FOLLOWING DECLARATION.)

I further declare that I am not related to the patient by blood, marriage, or adoption, and, to the best of my knowledge, I am not entitled to any part of his/her estate under a will now existing or by operation of law.

Signature: _____

Signature: _____

I further declare that I am not related to the patient by blood, marriage, or adoption, and, to the best of my knowledge, I am not entitled to any part of his/her estate under a will now existing or by operation of law.

Signature: _____

Signature: _____

## STATUTORY FORM POWER OF ATTORNEY
## (MINNESOTA)

**§ 523.23. Statutory short form of general power of attorney; formal requirements; joint agents.**

**Subdivision 1. Form.**

The use of the following form in the creation of a power of attorney is lawful, and, when used, it shall be construed in accordance with the provisions of sections 523.23 and 523.24:

**Notice:** THE POWERS GRANTED BY THIS DOCUMENT ARE BROAD AND SWEEPING. THEY ARE DEFINED IN SECTION 523.24 IF YOU HAVE ANY QUESTIONS ABOUT THESE POWERS, OBTAIN COMPETENT ADVICE. THE USE OF ANY OTHER OR DIFFERENT FORM OF POWER OF ATTORNEY DESIRED BY THE PARTIES IS ALSO PERMITTED. THIS POWER OF ATTORNEY MAY BE REVOKED BY YOU IF YOU LATER WISH TO DO SO. THIS POWER OF ATTORNEY AUTHORIZES THE ATTORNEY-IN-FACT TO ACT FOR YOU BUT DOES NOT REQUIRE THAT HE OR SHE DO SO.

Know All Men by These Presents, which are intended to constitute a STATUTORY SHORT FORM POWER OF ATTORNEY pursuant to Minnesota Statutes, section 523.23:

That I _____

_____

_____(insert name and address of the principal) do hereby appoint

_____

_____

_____

(insert name and address of the attorney-in-fact, or each attorney-in-fact, if more than one is designated) my attorney(s)-in-fact to act (jointly):

**Note:** If more than one attorney-in-fact is designated and the principal wishes each attorney-in-fact alone to be able to exercise the power conferred, delete the word "jointly." Failure to delete the word "jointly" will require the attorneys-in-fact to act unanimously.)

**First:** In my name, place and stead in any way which I myself could do, if I were personally present, with respect to the following matters as each of them is defined in section 523.24:

[To grant to the attorney-in-fact any of the following powers, make a check or "x" in the line in front of each power being granted. To delete any of the following powers, do not make a check or "x" in the line in front of the power. You may, but need not, cross out each power being deleted with a line drawn through it (or in similar fashion). Failure to make a check or "x" in the line in front of the power will have the effect of deleting the power unless the line in front of the power of (o) is checked or x-ed.]

Check or "x"

_____ (A)  real property transactions;
_____ (B)  tangible personal property transactions;
_____ (C)  bond, share, and commodity transactions;
_____ (D)  banking transactions;
_____ (E)  business operating transactions;
_____ (F)  insurance transactions;
_____ (G)  beneficiary transactions;
_____ (H)  gift transactions;
_____ (I)  fiduciary transactions;
_____ (J)  claims and litigation;
_____ (K)  family maintenance;
_____ (L)  benefits from military service;
_____ (M)  records, reports, and statements;
_____ (N)  all other matters;
_____ (O)  all of the powers listed in (A) through (N) above.

**Second:** [You must indicate below whether or not this power of attorney will be effective if you become incompetent. Make a check or "x" in the line in front of the statement that expresses your intent.]

_____ This power of attorney shall continue to be effective if I become incompetent. It shall not be affected by my later disability or incompetency.

_____ This power of attorney shall not be effective if I become incompetent.

**Third:** [You must indicate below whether or not this power of attorney authorizes the attorney-in-fact to transfer your property directly to himself or herself. Make a check or "x" in the line in front of the statement that expresses your intent.]

_____ This power of attorney authorizes the attorney-in-fact to transfer property directly to himself or herself.

_____ This power of attorney does not authorize the attorney-in-fact to transfer property directly to himself or herself.

In Witness Whereof I have hereunto signed my name this __ _____ day of _____ , 19 ____ .

_____
*(Signature of Principal)*

(Acknowledgment)

Specimen Signature of Attorney(s)-in-Fact

_____  _____

_____  _____

| APPENDIX 4 |
|:---:|

# FINANCIAL DATA SHEETS

Estate Planning for: _____
Self—Legal name in full

Date: _____

| **Personal** |
|:---|

Prior name(s) used: _____

_____

Current marital status: _____

Spouse's name _____

Previous marriages/dates of divorce: _____

_____

Primary residence (address): _____

_____

_____

Secondary residence (address): _____

_____

_____

Foreign residence, if ever (address): _____

_____

Resided while married in community property state, if ever:

_____

Business or profession: _____

_____

Business address: _____

_____

_____

Birth date: _____

Birth place: _____

_____

Citizenship: _____

Date naturalized: _____

Social security number: _____

_____

Military (yes/no): _____

Branch of service: _____

Dates of service: _____

Serial #: _____

Final rank: _____

_____

**Children**, name, address, date of birth/death (if applicable)

1. _____

_____

2. _____

_____

3. _____

_____

4. _____

_____

5. _____

_____

6. _____

_____

## Grandchildren, name, address, date of birth

1. _____

_____

2. _____

_____

3. _____

_____

4. _____

_____

5. _____

_____

6. _____

_____

7. _____

_____

8. _____

_____

## Professional organizations providing death benefits

Name (address): _____

_____

Death benefits provided: _____

_____

Credit cards in effect: _____

_____

Insurance provided (indicate type): _____

_____

_____

Name (address): _____

_____

Death benefits provided: _____

_____

Credit cards in effect: _____

_____

Insurance provided (indicate type): _____

_____

_____

Name (address): _____

_____

Death benefits provided: _____

_____

Credit cards in effect: _____

_____

Insurance provided (indicate type): _____

_____

_____

## Professional advisors

Lawyer: _____

Address: _____

### *Dying May Be Hazardous to Your Wealth*

Phone: _____

Accountant: _____
Address: _____
Phone: _____

Other tax professional: _____
Address: _____
Phone: _____

Financial planner: _____
Address: _____
Phone: _____

Stockbroker: _____
Address: _____
Phone: _____

Stockbroker #2: _____
Address: _____
Phone: _____

Insurance agent: _____
Address: _____
Phone: _____

Insurance agent #2: _____
Address: _____
Phone: _____

## Prior estate planning

Presently in effect:

I have a will  ❏yes  ❏no

Dated: _____

Prepared by: _____

Located: _____


Codicils, date: _____

Prepared by: _____

Located: _____


I have a trust(s)  ❏yes  ❏no

Prepared by: _____

_____

Witnesses: _____

_____

Located: _____

Powers of attorney, dates: _____

Prepared by: _____

Located: _____

_____

Medical instructions, date: _____

_____

If a court of law is in a position to adjudicate the continuance of life support devices I want you to know that my personal feelings are:_____

_____

Prepared by: _____

Voided wills and trusts, dated (indicate method of destroying—torn, burned, republished new document: _____

_____

_____

_____

## History of gift giving

Gifts over $3,000 prior to 1981: _____

_____

_____

_____

Dates: _____

Donees: _____

Property transferred: _____

Tax return filed (date): _____

Taxes paid: _____

_____

_____

Gifts over $10,000 after 1981: _____

_____

_____

Dates: _____

_____

Donees: _____

_____

Type of property transferred: _____

_____

Tax return filed (date): _____

_____

Taxes paid: _____

_____

_____

## Financial goals

Prioritize goals from 1 to 10 with 10 being most important:

❑ Protecting my spouse

❑ Tax-saving estate

❑ Tax savings—income

❑ Dividing assets fairly

❑ Dividing assets equally

❑ Helping my children

❑ Helping my grandchildren

❑ Giving to charity

❑ Disowning

❑ Protecting real estate for the family

❑ Preserving the family business

❑ Other

## Synopsis of will and trust

Executors, names and addresses:

1. _____

_____

2. _____

_____

3. _____

_____

Trustees, names and addresses:

1. _____

_____

2. _____

_____

3. _____

_____

Guardians, names and addresses:

1. _____

_____

2. _____

_____

3. _____

_____

Beneficiaries of will, names and addresses:

1. _____

_____

2. _____

_____

3. _____

_____

<u>Beneficiaries of trusts, names and addresses:</u>

1. _____

_____

2. _____

_____

3. _____

_____

<u>Successors, names and addresses:</u>

1. _____

_____

2. _____

_____

3. _____

_____

<u>Successor executors:</u> _____

_____

<u>Successor trustees:</u> _____

_____

<u>Successor guardians:</u> _____

_____

<u>Successor beneficiaries:</u> _____

_____

Disinherited persons: _____

_____

Conditional bequests: _____

_____

Legacies of tangible property (type and beneficiary): _____

_____

_____

## Documents

Documents on file, date, location: _____

_____

Tax returns—income: _____

_____

Tax returns—gift: _____

_____

Prior will: _____

Present will: _____

_____

Prior trusts: _____

Present trusts: _____

_____

Appraisals: _____

_____

Copyrights: _____

_____

Trademarks: _____

_____

Corporate books: _____

*Financial Data Sheets*

Military papers: _____

_____

Cemetery deeds, block and lot #: _____

_____

Safe deposit boxes—location and key: _____

_____

_____

Bank books: _____

_____

Brokerage statements: _____

_____

Other financial statements: _____

_____

Debt documents: _____

_____

Birth certificate: _____

_____

Passport: _____

_____

Marital documents: _____

_____

_____

Divorce documents: _____

_____

Insurance policies: _____

_____

Pension documents: _____

_____

## Burial wishes

(NOTE: Prepaid burial programs require that you give an amount of money or a whole life insurance policy to the funeral home. Recent IRS rulings have designated the growth on those policies and accounts taxable to you in each year you live. On the other hand, Medicaid exempts burial contracts or $2,500 of cash for burial expenses from spenddown if you go into a nursing home.)

I wish for:

❑ Burial in the earth

❑ Placement in a crypt

❑ Cremation

My place of burial should be: _____

_____

My coffin, casket, or urn should be: _____

_____

My monument, grave marker or head stone should be: ___

_____

My ashes should be scattered: _____

_____

My funeral services should be: _____

_____

My memorial services should be: _____

_____

Notify, if you can: _____

_____

I wish my body to be donated to: _____

_____

I wish specific body parts to be donated to: _____

_____

My donor card is located: _____

_____

If there is scientific reason, I wish an autopsy be performed: ___

_____

## Financial Family Tree

Construct your Financial Family Tree in the space provided below with yourself as the "trunk" of the tree, construct upper branches—those individuals who you expect to inherit from, whether parents, siblings or other. Then indicate the "roots," those individuals who you plan to leave assets to. On the drawing itself, you don't need to indicate specific property or amounts. These details will, of course, be included in your will or trusts.

**Congratulations—You've done a great job!**

# APPENDIX 5

# ESTATE AND GIFT TAX SCHEDULE

| Unified Rate Schedule | | | |
|---|---|---|---|
| Column A | Column B | Column C | Column D Rate of tax on excess over amount in column A |
| Taxable amount over | Taxable amount not over | Tax on amount in column A | |
| | | | (Percent) |
| 0 | $10,000 | 0 | 18 |
| $10,000 | 20,000 | $1,800 | 20 |
| 20,000 | 40,000 | 3,800 | 22 |
| 40,000 | 60,000 | 8,200 | 24 |
| 60,000 | 80,000 | 13,000 | 26 |
| 80,000 | 100,000 | 18,200 | 28 |
| 100,000 | 150,000 | 23,800 | 30 |
| 150,000 | 250,000 | 38,800 | 32 |
| 250,000 | 500,000 | 70,800 | 34 |
| 500,000 | 750,000 | 155,800 | 37 |
| 750,000 | 1,000,000 | 248,300 | 39 |
| 1,000,000 | 1,250,000 | 345,800 | 41 |
| 1,250,000 | 1,500,000 | 448,300 | 43 |
| 1,500,000 | 2,000,000 | 555,800 | 45 |
| 2,000,000 | 2,500,000 | 780,800 | 49 |
| 2,500,000 | 3,000,000 | 1,025,800 | 53 |
| 3,000,000 | 3,500,000 | 1,290,800 | 55 |

# APPENDIX 6

# LIABILITIES

(Include: mortgages, personal loans, credit cards, car loans, business loans, moral obligations, pledges to charity.)

_____

_____

_____

_____

_____

_____

_____

_____

_____

_____

_____

_____

_____

_____

_____

_____

_____

_____

_____

_____

_____

_____

_____

_____

# ASSETS

(Include: cash assets, stock money funds, checking accounts, savings accounts, stocks, bonds, collateralized mortgage obligations, treasury bills, bonds and notes, municipal bonds, anticipation notes, mutual funds, unit trusts, residential real estate, commerical real estate, public limited partnerships, private limited partnerships, art, antiques, jewelry, family business evaluations, homeowners insurance, tenants insurance, car insurance, life with cash value insurance, life term only insurance, mortgages held, notes held.)

_____

_____

_____

_____

_____

_____

_____

_____

_____

_____

_____

_____

_____

_____

_____

_____

_____

_____

_____

_____

# The Most Common Planned Giving Instruments

| Type of Gift | Form of Gift | Size of Gift | Benefits to Donor | Benefits to Charity |
|---|---|---|---|---|
| 1. Outright gifts | Cash<br>Securities<br>Real Estate<br>Insurance Policies | Unlimited | 100% deductible for income tax (up to 50% of adjusted gross income) for tax payers who itemize. | Funds are available for immediate use by the charity. |
| 2. Charitable Lead trusts | Cash<br>Securities<br>Real Estate | Usually $100,000 or more | Allows property to be passed to others with little or no shrinkage due to taxes. | Provides current income for period of at least 10 years. |
| 3. Life Income gifts, Irrevocable | | | | |
| A. Gift annuities | Cash<br>Securities | $1,000 minimum | Guaranteed, fixed income. Excellent tax deduction. | Provides future money for charity. Minimal administrative work and costs. |

| Type of Gift | Form of Gift | Size of Gift | Benefits to Donor | Benefits to Charity |
|---|---|---|---|---|
| B. Deferred payment gift annuities | Cash Securities | $1,000 minimum | Tax deduction during high income years. Guaranteed retirement income. | Same as gift annuity |
| C. Pooled income fund agreements | Cash Appreciated Securities | $2,000 minimum | Variable income that may provide hedge for inflation. No capital gains tax liability on gift. Tax deduction when gift is made. | Assures future funding for work of the charity. |
| D. Charitable Remainder Unitrusts | Cash Securities Real Estate | Usually $50,000 minimum | Same as Pooled Income Fund plus: Can be tailored to donor's situation. Permits deferred income if desired. Excellent for gifts of real estate. | Assures substantial future funding for work of the charity. Donor or charity may select Trustee. Charity may be able to use trust as collateral for loans. |

| Type of Gift | Form of Gift | Size of Gift | Benefits to Donor | Benefits to Charity |
|---|---|---|---|---|
| E. Charitable Remainder Annuity Trusts | Cash Securities | Usually $50,000 minimum | Fixed income. Tax deduction in year gift is made. No capital gains tax on appreciated gift. May provide tax-free income. | Same as Unitrusts. |
| 4. Revocable Charitable Trusts | Cash Securities Real Estate | Usually $50,000 minimum | All or part of amount placed in trust is available if need by donor. Removes work and worry of managing assets. | Very high percentage of revocable trusts are not revoked, thus giving promise of future funding for work of charity. |
| 5. Insurance Policies A. When charity is made owner and beneficiary of continuing policy | | Unlimited | Income tax deduction for value of policy when transferred. Premium payments deducted as gift. Donor makes large gift in future at small cost now. | Upon death of insured, charity will receive face value of policy. |

| Type of Gift | Form of Gift | Size of Gift | Benefits to Donor | Benefits to Charity |
|---|---|---|---|---|
| B. Giving paid-up policies | | Unlimited | Tax deduction based on current value of policy. | Charity may keep policy and receive face value upon death of insured. Charity may borrow on policy. Charity may cash in the policy. |
| C. Name charity as beneficiary but not as owner | | Unlimited | Enables donor to make large future gift at small cost. Donor may change beneficiary later. Donor may borrow on policy. | Upon death of insured, charity will receive face value of policy. |

(Special Note: Life insurance may also be sued to replenish the donor's estate for amounts given for a life income gift. Donor receives life income. Gives enough to someone else each year to pay premiums of life insurance policy on the donor. Upon death of donor, charity receives life income gift; family or others receive insurance proceeds—double mileage!)

**6. Bequests**

Anything one owns at the time of death may be passed on to the charity or anyone else through one's last will and testament. All forms of life income gifts listed above (Section 3) may be made in testamentary form to benefit family or friends and then will become available for use by the charity.

# INDEX